Writing to Learn

IN POLITICAL SCIENCE

Anne Michaels Edwards

D1301098

McGraw-Hill Primis
Custom Publishing

Boston   Burr Ridge, IL   Dubuque, IA   Madison, WI   New York   San Francisco
St. Louis   Bangkok   Bogotá   Caracas   Lisbon   London   Madrid   Mexico City   Milan
New Delhi   Paris   Seoul   Singapore   Sydney   Taipei   Toronto

McGraw-Hill Higher Education

A Division of The McGraw-Hill Companies

Writing to Learn in Political Science

1 2 3 4 5 6 7 8 9 0 DOC DOC 0 9 8 7 6 5 4 3 2 1

ISBN 0-07-243780-4

Primis Custom Publishing Editor: Beth Kundert
Printer/Binder: R.R. Donnelley & Sons Company

CONTENTS

ACKNOWLEDGMENTS

My thanks, as always to Mark, my *sine qua non*. And also to my mother, the late Maggie Ruback, who taught me how to read, write, live, love, and laugh. As Abraham Lincoln said, "All I am or hope to be I owe to my Mother."

Anne Michaels Edwards

1

INTRODUCTION

The purpose of this book is, quite simply, to teach you how to write political science essays. It is based largely on the premise that one of the best ways for a student to understand a topic is to be required to write about it. Most of the work in a political science class involves reading assigned material, thinking about it, and then writing about it—whether on an exam or in an essay written outside of class. This book is intended to make all three of those activities easier. However, this book is not for political science students only. While it should prove helpful in any political science class, regardless of teacher, subject, or textbook, you will be able to apply many of the guidelines to almost any paper or essay exam you are assigned in almost any college course.

There is so much about writing that a student needs to know, and so little time for an instructor to teach it. Most teachers want to focus on their subject (in this case, political science) and not on the task of writing. Although this book is not intended as a substitute for the instructor, it can be a valuable supplement for anyone enrolled in a political science course. If you have taken one or more political science classes already, then you may already know some of what is in this book. While the emphasis is on the kind of essays typically assigned in introductory political science classes, most of these same kinds of essays are assigned in upper-level courses as well.

If this is your first political science class, many of the names and theories will be unfamiliar to you. I have tried to include as many of them as possible in the glossary. However, don't be intimidated by things you don't know. As you are reading this book, should you come across a name, concept, or word you aren't familiar with, look it up in the glossary. In most instances, you will not need to know the people or the theories mentioned in order to understand the point being made.

This is meant to be a practical book. While your instructor may make use of this book in class, it is intended to be used with no interpretation or explanation necessary. Almost every political science class involves writing assignments of varying difficulty. *Writing to Learn* is meant to help you fulfill these assignments better, and, with luck, to earn a good grade in the process. The kinds of essays covered in Chapters 3, 4, and 5 are usually found only on examinations, in book reviews, or in case briefs. Papers assigned by your instructor will probably be like those discussed in Chapters 6, 7, and 8. Even if your instructor doesn't assign out-of-class papers, chances are good that on exams, quizzes, or in-class essays, you will be required to write one or more of these kinds of essays.

Chapters 3 through 7 will guide you through several different types of essays, beginning with the simplest summaries, which demonstrate knowledge and understanding, and progressing through essays that require the application of theories to new situations, the analysis of the arguments used, the evaluation of those arguments, and finally, the synthesis of several theories or arguments.[1] One chapter is devoted to each of these levels of knowledge, illustrating the kind of reasoning necessary and helping you to write an essay at that level. Clearly, you must accomplish the easier levels of reasoning before you can progress to the ones that are more difficult.

What this means is that, while each chapter can be used independently ("My instructor assigned an evaluative essay, I'd better read Chapter 6"), each chapter builds on the previous chapters. For example, you can't write an evaluative essay until you can first write a summary as well as an analysis of what you want to evaluate. Therefore, your best bet is to read the book straight through. However, for those of you who won't do that because of time constraints or general disinclination, some hints follow in the section below.

Writing an essay is a good way to develop your ideas on a topic. By attempting to express an idea in your own words, you gain a deeper and more complete understanding than if you merely read what someone else has written. Thus, political science is something you *do*—it is not a collection of facts to be learned or equations to be applied. When you

---

[1] I am obviously indebted to Benjamin Bloom, et al., *Taxonomy of Educational Objectives: The Classifications of Educational Goals. Handbook I: Cognitive Domain* (New York: Longman Publishing, 1980).

"do political science," as we like to say, you are actively reading, thinking, and writing. And this is the only way to "do" political science. No one can "teach" it to you—you have to "learn" it yourself. You must, then, take these words about teaching to heart:

> It is obvious that teaching is a very special art, sharing with only two other arts—agriculture and medicine—an exceptionally important characteristic. A doctor may do many things for his patient, but in the final analysis it is the patient himself who must get well—grow in health. The farmer does many things for his plants or animals, but in the final analysis it is they that must grow in size and excellence. Similarly, although the teacher may help his students in many ways, it is the student himself who must do the learning. Knowledge must grow in his mind if learning is to take place.[2]

HOW TO USE THIS BOOK

For those students unable to read this text in its entirety, the following overview should help to identify when and how each of the chapters will be most useful.

Chapter 2: Reading Political Science

This book begins in Chapter 2 with some helpful hints on how to read political science. You should certainly read this chapter before you read anything else. Because the content of a course is generally found in the readings, and because most often you are asked to write about something that you have read, it is very important that you read carefully and well. If you can't understand what you are reading, you can't write about it. Reading political science is probably unlike reading anything else you encounter. It requires slow reading, extensive rereading, and can be made easier by using certain techniques. This chapter won't make reading political science easy, but it should make it easier.

Chapter 3: Writing for Understanding

If your instructor is giving an essay exam, *be sure* you read Chapter 3 on writing for understanding (and also see Appendix A on taking exams). Whatever else an instructor asks you to do, he is sure to ask you to *summarize* some essay or theory. (Of course, you will probably be asked

---

[2] Mortimer J. Adler and Charles Van Doren, *How to Read a Book* (New York: Touchstone Books, 1972), pp. 12–13.

to do more than that, but *at least* you must be able to do this much.) For example, a typical question on an Introduction to Political Science exam might read:

> In *On Liberty*, John Stuart Mill argues that freedom of speech should be almost unlimited. What are the four reasons he gives to support that conclusion?

Any question that asks for a definition also requires a summary. For example:

> Describe the basic principles of parliamentary government.

> Explain the principle of distributive justice.

> What are Aristotle's six forms of political government?

> What is the state for, according to Plato?

While these may be only the *first* part of the question (for example, the question about Plato may go on to ask if you agree with him), without being able to put the arguments and theories into your own words, you will not be able to answer the rest of the question. You may also be asked to brief a case (that is, summarize a court decision), or write a book review. Each of these requires the ability to identify the important aspects of the work and put them into your own words.

Chapter 4: Writing for Application

If your instructor asks you to *apply* some theory to a new situation, head straight for Chapter 4. An application question typically looks something like this:

> Briefly describe the Milgram experiment and findings. How do these findings help explain how the Holocaust could have happened?

Notice that first it asks you to summarize both the experiment and the conclusions drawn (which is why you need to understand Chapter 3 first). Then it asks you to apply Milgram's findings to a particular example. Other examples, which would also require you to first summarize a theory (although they may not explicitly say so), are these:

> Give two examples of political behavior.

> Define "validity" as it pertains to opinion poll questions. Give an example of an "invalid" question.

> Describe the four types of interest groups and give examples of each.

First you must say, "Here is what the theory or definition is," and then, "And here is how that applies to such-and-such, or here's an example of it." You may also be asked to explain how a given law or statute applies to a particular case. As you can see, you are unlikely to have any question that is *purely* summary or application.

Chapter 5: Writing for Analysis

If your instructor asks you to *analyze* an argument, Chapter 5 will show you how to examine ideas and theories and break them into their component parts. The chapter talks about argument form and common argumentative mistakes and discusses how to separate facts from opinions, necessary from probable conclusions, and assumptions from logical conclusions. Analysis involves not only explaining an author's conclusion, but also his reasons for believing his conclusion and how he argues for his conclusion. An analysis question might ask:

> The Electoral College is a unique element of government and often-debated feature of the United States Constitution. How does it work? Why did the framers of the Constitution create it?

Not only must you be able to say what the Electoral College is and how it works (summary), but you must be prepared to analyze the reasons the framers of the Constitution gave for why they created it. Other examples include:

> What is John Stuart Mill's argument regarding the connection between justice and utility?

> How does John Rawls argue for the legitimacy of his two principles of justice?

> Why did John Locke favor a divided government and a right to revolution?

Other kinds of analyses you may be asked to write include policy analyses (in which you are asked to explain the relative costs and benefits of different government decisions) and political analyses (in which you are asked to analyze the political process itself.)

Chapter 6: Writing for Evaluation

Turn to Chapter 6 when you must write the most common essay assigned, the *evaluative essay*. An evaluative essay requires that you first summarize and analyze an argument (or a policy), and then evaluate it. Is the author right? Why or why not? Do her reasons support her conclusion? In an evaluative essay, you are essentially arguing for a position. Clearly, if you have not learned to write the earlier types of essays, this kind of essay can be impossibly hard and largely incomprehensible. The following are typical evaluative questions:

> Explain Robert Nozick's reasoning that the "night-watchman" state is the only one that does not violate individual rights. Do you agree?

> What is John Locke's argument that we have a right to own personal property? What are the strengths of this view? The weaknesses?

> In *The Federalist No. 10,* James Madison argued that unequal distribution of property is the most common and durable source of political factions. Do you think his reasoning is sound?

Chapter 7: Writing for Synthesis

If none of the earlier chapters match what your instructor has asked you to do, turn to Chapter 7—*synthesis essays. Synthesis* involves bringing together parts and elements of several theories to create a new whole that requires original thinking. A synthesis essay may involve comparing and contrasting several theories or constructing your own position on a topic and defending it. A typical synthesis question might read like this:

> Compare and contrast single member, winner-take-all districts and multiple member, proportional systems of democracy.

> How would you relate Aristotle's views on political society to Plato's and your own?

> Which is the better form of government—direct democracy or representative democracy? Provide an argument to support your position.

> Choose a problem you perceive in your state and write a letter to your congressman explaining what the problem is and how you think it should be resolved.

These questions ask you to create your *own* argument for a particular conclusion. Notice that synthesis essays, like evaluative essays, are argumentative. That is, you are arguing that your theory is the correct one. This is, in some ways, the hardest kind of essay to write. Although some students instinctively want to take the best of several theories to make one they feel is better, many find it hard to think creatively in this way.

However, remember, you can't expect to write a good synthesis essay if you cannot write a good summary, application, analysis, and evaluation.

Chapter 8: Using Research in a Political Science Paper

If you are expected to do research for your paper, read Chapter 8. You will probably also need to read Chapter 6 and possibly Chapter 7, since most research papers may also be evaluative or synthesis essays. And, of course, you should probably understand Chapter 5, in order to analyze what you read. In general, I tell students that if they have read anything other than their textbook in preparing their essays, then they need to follow the guidelines for a research essay. Chapter 8 covers the use of sources and quotations and the proper form for footnotes and bibliographies.

Chapter 9: Putting Pencil to Paper (or Fingers to Keyboard)

Chapter 9 contains suggestions on how to get started as well as a discussion of the mechanics of the essay. There is advice about following directions, writing the kind of essay assigned, using the right paper, margins, fonts, and so on. Chapter 9 also emphasizes the need for rewriting, rewriting, and rewriting some more! While most of the information about first drafts is in the respective chapters, this chapter offers guidance on how to avoid common mistakes (like sexist language and some common fallacies), as well as editing and proofreading. At the very least, you should read Chapter 9 before writing any essay.

Appendixes

The text concludes with three appendixes. Appendix A has some helpful hints on how to take exams. Appendix B contains a bibliography of political science resources especially helpful to introductory students (like *The American Political Dictionary*[3], *The Social Sciences Index*, and various reference works that are easily accessible). It is not a very long list; rather, it includes just a few of the very best, most common and easily available resources you might use in the course of writing a political science essay. Appendix C is a glossary of words, theories, names, movements, and so on that you might come into contact with in your political science course. In addition to key terms (which appear in boldface type in the chapters), it also includes brief definitions or designations of all the people and theories mentioned in the book.

---

[3] Plano, Jack C., and Milton Greenburg, *The American Political Dictionary*, 10th edition. (Fort Worth: Harcourt Brace Jovanovich, 1966).

Now you should have all the information you need—either to begin at the beginning and work straight through to the end, or else to go straight to the relevant chapter. Good luck!

2

READING POLITICAL SCIENCE

Before you can write intelligibly about a subject, you must first *understand* the subject. Since most of the writing you are asked to do in political science classes will be about something you have read, it is essential that you learn to read political science well. Reading political science is different from most other reading you do. Unlike some of your other college textbooks, you cannot skim a political science essay for the main facts or details. You must read much more slowly than you would, say, a magazine or a novel. Political science writing is what we like to call *dense* reading. That is, there are many ideas in a compact space. While you could probably get the sense of a novel by reading only every second or third paragraph, this kind of tactic would never work in political science. Sentence structure is often complex, and the topic may be one that you have never thought deeply about or one that you do not find particularly interesting. In addition, the fact that a political science essay is often presenting an argument or explaining someone else's argument means that you must pay close attention to every part of the essay.

Also, some essays were written hundreds or even thousands of years ago. They rely on words, ideas, and assumptions that may have been clear at the time they were written, but are no longer clear to the modern reader. Some essays were written in other languages and have been translated. Sometimes the translations are bad ones; sometimes the translations are so accurate that they reflect the complexity of the original language a little too well for American readers (this is particularly true of some translations from German); and sometimes the original essay, whether in a foreign language or not, was not well written. It is sad, but true, that many essays are poorly written, contain confused or faulty arguments, and/or rest on assumptions and ideas that are either questionable or downright wrong.

Don't be surprised if you don't understand an essay the first time you read it. Don't even be surprised if you don't understand all of it the second time around. Reading political science requires a great deal of patience, concentration, and perseverance. You must read, reread, and then reread some more. Like any other skill, your ability to read political science will improve with practice.

TECHNIQUES FOR READING POLITICAL SCIENCE

While political science can be difficult reading, it is not impossible. This section presents some techniques that will make the task ahead of you easier.

Give Yourself Enough Time

Read the entire section or essay in one sitting. If you try to read your homework in 10- or 15-minute segments, you will not succeed. Because a political science essay often proposes a line of reasoning, if you stop in the middle you run the risk of forgetting what came before. While this is not fatal if you are reading a novel or a magazine article, it is for a political science essay. Not only do you have to read the whole essay, but you have to *understand* it too. A large part of that understanding involves following the process of the author's reasoning. So give yourself plenty of time to read completely through the assignment.

Use All Available Study Aids

If your reading is from a textbook, make good use of all the study aids the author or editor offers. Read the preface or introduction to the book. Read chapter and essay introductions or summaries. Examine the study questions to get an idea of what the important points probably are. Take advantage of any section headings, margin notes, and boxed passages if your textbook offers them. Make liberal use of the glossary, if there is one, and the index. If the book has a detailed table of contents, study it. Skim the reading first to spot any headings or emphasized passages. All of these are instructional features that can help you read the book more easily. Many of the readings that you will be assigned will contain one or more of these features. Take advantage of them!

Grant All Ideas a Fair Hearing

One good rule to follow when you are reading is what is called the **principle of charity**. If your instructor has asked you to read an essay, he most likely thinks that there is something valuable to be learned from the essay. Be charitable. Give the authors the benefit of the doubt. Even if you think they are wrong, try to be very clear about *what* you think they are saying and *why* you think they are mistaken. Grant all ideas a fair hearing, even if (especially if) you don't agree with them. People have the most trouble understanding and remembering ideas they disagree with, so this is something to work on.

Read and Reread

You can rarely read a political science essay just once and completely understand it. This kind of writing demands careful, slow, and repeated reading. You will probably have to read the entire essay at least twice, and some individual passages you may need to read several more times. Reread as often as you need to, to understand what the author is saying. However, don't spend so much time rereading a passage that you get discouraged. If you really can't understand a particular section or passage, flag it and come back to it later. After you have read further, you may find that your understanding has improved, and you can now reread passages you didn't understand with more comprehension.

Change Your Surroundings

If you are experiencing a great deal of frustration or difficulty with your reading, consider finding a new place to read. If you are tired, distracted, uncomfortable, hungry, thirsty, or whatever, you may have difficulties with your reading. The better you can make the atmosphere, the better your comprehension is likely to be.

Read Actively

You must read actively—that is, you must be constantly asking yourself: What is the main point? Why did the author just say that? What are the author's reasons for believing this? Do I agree or disagree with this point? Keep a pencil, a highlighter, a pad of sticky notes, or a note pad handy. Mark passages that seem important, or passages that you don't understand. However, don't highlight every sentence! In fact, don't underline or highlight at all on your first reading, except to mark passages you don't understand. Only on the second reading should you begin to mark up the text (and then only if you own the book); otherwise take notes. Also, annotate as you read. Comments may be as simple as "huh?" or "yes!" They may be your thoughts on why the author is wrong, or they may indicate how what the author says connects with something else that you've read. Use your notes to ask questions, to mark passages you don't understand, or to indicate where you agree or disagree and what you think are the significant parts of the essay.

Keep a Dictionary Handy

Merriam-Webster's Collegiate Dictionary[1] is a good comprehensive dictionary that can often be found on sale for a reasonable price. A paperback pocket dictionary probably will not be adequate. Many scholars tend to use large and sometimes obscure words. Occasionally you can get the meaning from the context of the essay, but often you can't. So using a good dictionary is critical.

Stop and Summarize What You Have Read

After you finish a section or a page, pause and see if you can restate what the author is saying in your own words. If you cannot do so, then you do not understand what you have read. Summarizing is described at length in Chapter 3, but here is a short overview. As you read, regularly stop, close your eyes, and mentally summarize the main points of what you have read. If you are ambitious, actually writing your summary down is even better, since it helps you remember what you've read. This does not mean merely paraphrasing some sentences or the section headings. It means figuring out what the *most important* parts of the essay or argument are and restating them so that you know that you understand them—and are not merely parroting what you have read.

Look for the Essay's Main Points

On your first reading of an essay, you should be looking for the author's **conclusions**. Ask yourself, What is the author trying to prove? Just grasping the main points is a large part of the battle. Don't try to understand every sentence the first time through. If there are passages or details that you find particularly difficult even after reading them several times, skip over them and go on. Perhaps by the next time through

---

[1] *Merriam-Webster's Collegiate Dictionary*, 10th Edition (Springfield, Massachusetts: Merriam-Webster, Inc., 1997).

you'll understand them better. If you spend too much time trying to fig-ure out the fine points, you may completely miss the main points.

Identify the Essay's Premises

Once you understand the point or points the author is trying to prove, you need to figure out what her *reasons* are. On your second reading, ask yourself, *Why* does she think her conclusion is true? As a rule, a po-litical science essay offers a chain of ideas, in which some of the ideas (what we call the **premises**) are meant to provide reasons for believing another idea, the *conclusion*. The premises are usually (and should be) simpler, clearer, and more obvious than the conclusion. And the author should make the connection between the premises and the conclusion clear. Unfortunately, as you will eventually discover, this isn't always the case. The primary task in reading is to identify the author's premises and conclusion. If you don't catch them all on your first reading, you will understand more on your second reading.

Talk to Your Instructor

If you still do not understand an essay after following all these sugges-tions, then you should consult your instructor. It may be that the essay you are reading is particularly difficult, complex, or confusing. Your instructor is one of your most important resources. Instructors, in gen-eral, *like* to talk about their subjects and are more than happy to help, clarify, or just chat about your readings.

Reading political science can be challenging! But developing this skill will be invaluable to you in many of your other classes, particularly those in the Humanities. The ability to read closely and carefully, to un-derstand not only what the author is trying to prove but also what her reasons are for her conclusions, transfers to many other fields, including economics, physics, medicine, law, and psychology, to name a few. Like any other skill such as playing the piano or working algebra prob-lems, spending time developing this skill will eventually make your reading easier. The more you do it, the simpler it gets, and the more en-joyable it becomes.

3

WRITING FOR UNDERSTANDING

At the most basic level of writing, instructors typically expect two things of a student: knowledge of previously learned material (i.e., names, dates, theories, concepts, and principles); and *understanding* of what has been learned. An **understanding essay** is essentially a summary or a paraphrase of an argument. You will often be required to write a summary of a theory on an essay exam, either as a separate question or as part of a question demanding analysis, application, or evaluation. You may also be asked to write a case brief (a summary of a court decision) or a book review (a summary of an entire book.) The ability to write a coherent summary of a theory is the first step in understanding it. If you can't summarize an argument or essay in a hundred words or so, then you don't understand it.

Suppose the following passage was part of your weekly reading from John Stuart Mill's *On Liberty*:

> The object of this Essay is to assert one very simple principle . . . that the sole end for which mankind are warranted, individually or collectively, in interfering with the liberty of action of any of their number, is self-protection. That the only purpose for which power can be rightfully exercised over any member of a civilized commu-

nity, against his will, is to prevent harm to others. His own good, either physical or moral, is not a sufficient warrant.[1]

If your instructor wants to test your knowledge of Mill's main point, then what he is asking for is simple repetition, as in this answer:

> The sole reason for which society is warranted in interfering with the liberty of action of any of their number, is to prevent harm to others. His own good, either physical or moral, is not a good reason.

If, however, your instructor is trying to determine whether you understand the Mill's theory, then merely repeating Mill's words will not be enough: You must express Mill's principle in your own words. Notice that although the previous answer did not entirely use Mill's exact words, still the words and phrases are much too close to Mill's original for the instructor to be certain that you understand what you have read. A better example of understanding would be this:

> According to Mill, the only reason you can interfere with a person's freedom is to prevent them from harming someone else. You can't force people to do things to prevent them from harming themselves or because you think it would be good for them.

Aside from some multiple-choice and matching questions on exams, instructors will rarely ask for mere *knowledge* of a theory, essay, or principle. In fact, even multiple-choice questions often require *understanding* as well. While an instructor will rarely have you write an essay *merely* showing understanding, almost every essay you write will *require* that you show understanding of some theory, essay, or principle. Thus, in order to write *any* kind of political science essay, you need to master the understanding essay first.

You show that you understand a theory or essay by using paraphrases and summaries. It is important that you understand the difference.

PARAPHRASING

Paraphrasing a passage means simply to put the ideas and thoughts of an author into your own words. That is, when you paraphrase, you show the meaning of the passage by presenting it in another form—that is, in other words. If your instructor asks you to define a principle, she is asking you to paraphrase the appropriate passage. In the examples

---

[1] John Stuart Mill, *On Liberty*, Chapter I, "Introductory" (London: Longman, Roberts & Green, 1869).

above, I paraphrased Mill's main point from *On Liberty*. Be careful, however, that you don't stick so closely to the author's words, syntax, and sentence structure that you are guilty of plagiarism, or presenting the author's writing—or wording very close to it—as your own. We will discuss plagiarism in depth in Chapter 8. The first example above commits plagiarism. You must always use your own words, whether on an exam or in an essay, no matter how inelegant they may be compared to the original. This is not only to avoid plagiarism, but also because only in that way can you demonstrate to your instructor that you understand the principle in question.

Consider the rest of the above passage from Mill's *On Liberty*:

The object of this Essay is to assert one very simple principle, as entitled to govern absolutely the dealings of society with the individual in the way of compulsion and control, whether the means used be physical force in the form of legal penalties, or the moral coercion of public opinion. That principle is, that the sole end for which mankind are warranted, individually or collectively, in interfering with the liberty of action of any of their number, is self-protection. That the only purpose for which power can be rightfully exercised over any member of a civilized community, against his will, is to prevent harm to others. His own good, either physical or moral, is not a sufficient warrant. He cannot rightfully be compelled to do or forbear because it will be better for him to do so, because it will make him happier, because, in the opinions of others, to do so would be wise, or even right. These are good reasons for remonstrating with him, or reasoning with him, or persuading him, or entreating him, but not for compelling him, or visiting him with any evil in case he do otherwise. To justify that, the conduct from which it is desired to deter him, must be calculated to produce evil to some one else. The only part of the conduct of any one, for which he is amenable to society, is that which concerns others. In the part which merely concerns himself, his independence is, of right, absolute. Over himself, over his own body and mind, the individual is sovereign.[2]

Here is a bad example of a paraphrase of this passage:

Mill says that the object of his essay is to assert one simple principle: that society and individuals are not justified in interfering with the liberty of action of an individual, except to prevent harm to oth-

---

[2] Mill, *On Liberty*, Chapter I.

> ers. His own good, whether physical or moral, is not a good reason. He cannot rightfully be forced to do or not to do something because it would be better for him to do so, because he would be happier, or because other people think it would be right for him to do so. The only part of our conduct that we have to answer to others for is that which involves others. In the part that merely concerns ourselves, our own minds and bodies, we should have total control.

This paraphrase is bad because it mimics Mill's words and syntax much too closely. The following is a better example of paraphrasing. It shows that the writer understands the passage in a way that the earlier example does not.

> Mill says that the only reason society can legitimately force people to do things or not to do things, against their will, is to prevent them from causing harm to others. If it is a matter that only involves the individual himself, then no one should interfere with him.

Notice that this paraphrase is true to the original—that is, it expresses the same ideas—but it uses words and sentence structure sufficiently different from the original that it is fairly clear that the passage has been understood.

SUMMARIZING

When you are asked to describe or explain an entire theory, argument, or essay, you need to write a **summary**. If you merely paraphrase every sentence, then you will end up with an essay as long as the original. A summary should be considerably shorter than the original. It is not a sentence-by-sentence paraphrase and it does not use the author's words, phrases, or sentence structure. In a summary, you are attempting to explain the essay's major points. This means that you must identify not only the author's *conclusions*, but also his reasons (his *premises*) for those conclusions. If your summary is too long, then you do not understand the essay well enough.

No matter what kind of essay you plan to write, you should write one or more summaries beforehand. Writing a very short summary will help you decide if you understand the argument or theory. If you are writing about a particular argument or theory, write a short (100–200 words) summary of the argument first. Simply passing your eyes over the page and underlining important passages does not guarantee that you understand what you have read. Remember when you summarize a passage or essay that you must identify the reasons an author gives for his views, as well as his conclusion.

Do not begin writing a summary until you have finished reading the entire essay or argument, and don't expect to be able to write a good summary after only one reading. Sometimes earlier passages cannot be completely understood without the connections made in later passages, and sometimes the main point isn't clear until the end of the essay. Be sure you understand what the author is trying to prove or accomplish before you begin your summary. Remember, you need to know more than just his conclusions. You need to be sure that you understand the reasons he gives for those conclusions as well. Getting to this point takes time—lots of patient reading and rereading.

As you read the essay you intend to summarize, jot down what seem to be the major points and premises. Then, when you are ready to begin writing the summary, close your book and write the summary from memory. If you find that you must constantly refer to the essay you are trying to summarize, then you do not yet understand the essay well enough. By not looking at the original essay, you will prevent unintended quoting and plagiarism and will force yourself to rely only on what you actually understand. Continual reference back to the original will probably result in mere paraphrasing of the original. When you paraphrase a passage sentence-by-sentence, you may understand each sentence individually but not the context—how the premises fit together to prove the conclusion.

Premises, remember, are the reasons the author gives for thinking her conclusions are true. The premises are generally simpler and clearer ideas that fit together in a particular way to provide proof or evidence for an idea—the conclusion—that is less obvious and probably less clear. Paraphrase is most often required when you are asked on an essay exam to define a term, principle, or theory. Another use of paraphrase comes in an essay when you are trying to lay out an author's premises and conclusions. You usually need to paraphrase the most important points, rather than simply summarize the whole argument.

The most important question you should ask yourself about any paraphrase or summary is this: Does my paraphrase/summary accurately reflect what the original essay or passage says? You need to be sure that anyone reading your paraphrase/summary will be able to understand the important points made by the author, even though he is unfamiliar with the original. That is, a paraphrase should convey *exactly* the same meaning as the original, although using different words and syntax. A summary should provide a much shorter, but still accurate, rendering of the entire argument or essay.

EXAMPLE

If your instructor asks you to write an "understanding essay," whether on an exam or as an out-of-class assignment, she will most often use one or more of these words: Explain, define, discuss, describe, or summarize. Often a question requiring understanding will begin, "What is . . ." or "What are . . . ." For example, the following is a possible essay exam question or essay topic that requires you to understand an essay, principle, or argument:

> In *On Liberty*, John Stuart Mill argues that freedom of speech should be almost unlimited. What are the four reasons he gives to support that conclusion?

The following is the passage from which your answer would be drawn.

> We have now recognised the necessity to the mental well-being of mankind (on which all their other well-being depends) of freedom of opinion, and freedom of the expression of opinion, on four distinct grounds; which we will now briefly recapitulate.
>
> First, if any opinion is compelled to silence, that opinion may, for aught we can certainly know, be true. To deny this is to assume our own infallibility.
>
> Secondly, though the silenced opinion be an error, it may, and very commonly does, contain a portion of truth; and since the general or prevailing opinion on any subject is rarely or never the whole truth, it is only by the collision of adverse opinions that the remainder of the truth has any chance of being supplied.
>
> Thirdly, even if the received opinion be not only true, but the whole truth; unless it is suffered to be, and actually is, vigorously and earnestly contested, it will, by most of those who receive it, be held in the manner of a prejudice, with little comprehension or feeling of its rational grounds. And not only this, but, fourthly, the meaning of the doctrine itself will be in danger of being lost, or enfeebled, and deprived of its vital effect on the character and conduct: the dogma becoming a mere formal profession, inefficacious for good, but cumbering the ground, and preventing the growth of any real and heartfelt conviction, from reason or personal experience.[3]

So what does the passage mean? This summary answers the essay question:

---

[3] Mill, *On Liberty*, Chapter II, "Of the Liberty of Thought and Discussion".

Mill says that there are four reasons for thinking that freedom of speech ("freedom of the expression of opinion" as he calls it) should be almost unlimited. First, he says, the idea we want to suppress may be true, and if we suppress it, we lose the chance of knowing the truth. Second, the idea we want to suppress may be partially true, and, again, if we suppress it, we will lose the chance of learning the truth. Third, even if our own opinion is true, if we don't allow people to express their disagreement with it, we will hold it as a prejudice—that is, we won't have good reasons for thinking it is true. Finally, even if our opinion is true, if we don't allow dissenting opinions to be heard, then the originally meaning of our idea will be lost.

This is a good summary because it does not mimic Mill's words or sentence structure too closely and it accurately reflects his main points in the passage.

When writing a summary, remember to ask yourself: Does my summary accurately reflect what the original essay or passage says? If not, try again. Be sure that you do not just paraphrase, or, worst of all, plagiarize, the author's own sentences. An instructor requests a summary when she wants to know whether you understand an essay or passage. Mere paraphrase or quotation does not show that you understand the argument.

4

WRITING FOR APPLICATION

Writing what I call an **application essay** is more difficult than merely knowing and understanding the theory that you are writing about. Of course, you have to understand the theory *first* (which is why you should master the understanding essay described in Chapter 3 first). To write an application essay, you need to take what you have learned in another context and apply it to a new situation.

This is a favorite type of essay exam question for many professors—applying a theory, court case, statute, or policy to a particular situation. For instance:

> Apply Socrates' argument in the *Crito*, that civil disobedience is never justified, to the practice of draft dodging.

Of course, Socrates never wrote about draft dodging, so you don't *know* what the correct answer is here, and no amount of studying your text will tell you. However, even though you can't be sure what Socrates would say, if you understand his position on civil disobedience, you should be able to make a pretty good guess as to what his answer would be to the question about draft dodging.

If this were an essay exam question, the following would be a sample answer:

> Socrates claims that since the state has been like a parent to him, he should not disobey it by escaping from prison. He says that by

choosing to live in Athens and to enjoy the benefits of living there, he has implicitly agreed to follow its laws. He could have left Athens and moved elsewhere, he could have worked to change the laws, or he could have chosen exile as his punishment. But he chose not to do any of those. Because of that, Socrates claims he has to abide by the laws of Athens—i.e. the jury's decision to execute him.

In the case of draft dodging, I think Socrates would say that it was wrong. Since those who want to avoid the draft have enjoyed the benefits of the U.S.—including education, national defense, police protection, and interstate highways—they are obligated to follow the rules. And the rules say that, if called upon, they have to help provide for the defense of the country.

Notice that the writer of this essay *first* states Socrates' position in her own words (that is, she does not merely quote him), and *then* she applies it to a new situation and comes up with an answer. Notice also that she doesn't merely say, "Socrates would say don't do it." She explains why he would say that—how his theory leads to that conclusion.

Here's another sample question:

A woman claims that she was sexually harassed by her employer. Her boss posts nude photographs of women on the door to his office, he repeatedly asks her about her sexual habits, and has made several obscene phone calls to her office phone. She has complained to her superiors, but nothing has been done. During this time she has received several promotions and pay raises. According to Title VII of the Civil Rights Act, has she been discriminated against?

To answer this question, you have to know not only what Title VII says, but also what kind of cases have been tried under it. Here is a possible answer.

Title VII of the Civil Rights Act prohibits discrimination in the workplace. The Supreme Court has decided that sexual harassment is a form of gender discrimination, so according to the most recent case law, yes, she has been discriminated against, and can sue under Title VII, even if she has not suffered any damage to her career.

These are fairly simple examples of applying something you already know to a new and different situation. Of course, application essays can be much more complicated. Entire books have been written on applying a particular moral theory to capital punishment, draft dodging, and abortion.

USING EXAMPLES

Another type of application essay or exam question asks you to provide **examples**. Any time you are asked to "give an example of," "show how," "demonstrate," or "illustrate," you are being asked to apply some theory or principle to a new situation. For example:

> Herbert Marcuse argues that the needs satisfied by advanced capitalist societies are, to a large extent, false needs. Explain and give two examples.

Here's a sample answer:

> Marcuse says that companies falsely stimulate the need for their products through advertising and the media. They basically convince people that if they want to "live the good life" they need to have certain products. When they show famous people using a particular product, or eating at a particular restaurant, or something like that, they are trying to persuade people that if they want to live like the celebrities, then they need to do the same thing. So people buy big TVs, new cars, expensive clothes, etc. even though they don't really need them. People don't really *need* to wear designer jeans— Levis or Wranglers would do. Most people who just drive around town don't *need* an SUV that is designed for driving off road. These are false needs which capitalism promotes. Marcuse says that this is essentially a form of social control. By convincing people they need these things, people will support capitalism—the idea that people should be able to make more and more and more money.

USING COUNTER-EXAMPLES

Another type of example you may be asked to provide in an application essay or exam is a **counter-example**—an example meant to show that a theory or principle is incorrect. Many people think that Mill's argument (presented in the last chapter) that freedom of speech should be almost unlimited is wrong. They say that hate speech is a good example of speech that we should not allow. The argument goes something like this.

> Mill argues that we should never prevent people from expressing their opinions. However, since we already know that racists are wrong, we don't need to allow them to express their opinions. Mill argues that we can benefit even from wrong opinions, but I think we have already benefited as much as we ever will. Allowing people to use hate speech incites others to violence, and deteriorates our soci-

ety. In addition, because hate speech causes harm to people, according to Mill's own argument (found in the first chapter of *On Liberty*), we as a society have a right to prevent them from causing that harm.

Mill, of course, wouldn't agree. While he agrees that we can interfere with people's freedom to prevent them from causing harm to others, he also believes that opinions don't cause harm (or at least, not the kind of harm he is talking about in Chapter I). In either case, this example should have taught you a valuable lesson about counter-examples. Just remember that a good counter-example must be *obviously* wrong. So this counter-example may not be very satisfactory.

CONCLUDING REMARKS

The key to providing either examples or counter-examples is to be sure that they very clearly show what you want. A good counter-example must show, to the satisfaction of most people anyway, that the theory is false. That is, it must be pretty clear that the consequences of accepting the theory are unacceptable. A good example, on the other hand, needs to clearly illustrate the theory or principle in question.

Even if you aren't asked to give an example or a counter-example, it is often wise to do so, particularly on essay exams. Examples and counter-examples are useful in making a theory or principle clearer and more understandable. Applying a theory or principle to new situations by creating examples shows a higher level of understanding than just explaining the theory, in the same way that (as I showed in the last chapter) summarizing a theory in your own words shows a higher level of understanding than merely repeating or quoting the author's original words.

5

WRITING FOR ANALYSIS

When your instructor asks you to provide an **analysis** of an essay, argument, or theory, he is not merely asking you to explain what the author is saying. To analyze an argument, you must not only understand the *content* of the argument, but you should also understand its *structure*. You must be able to break the argument down into its component parts and recognize the relationship between those parts. This means that you must not only understand each of the separate parts of the argument or theory, but you need to determine the connections and interactions between those parts. While you may also be asked to analyze a political policy (in which you are asked to explain the relative costs and benefits of different government decisions) or a political process, I concentrate here on argument analysis. In order to help you write for analysis, this chapter will show you how to distinguish conclusions from the premises that support them, **facts** from **opinions**, **necessary** from **probable conclusions**, and **assumptions** from logical conclusions. In addition, you will learn to detect unstated assumptions, logical **fallacies**, and **emotional language**.

ARGUMENTS

An **argument**, remember, is a set of statements, one of which is the conclusion and the rest of which are the premises. The premises are

25

supposed to give you reasons, evidence, or justification for believing that the conclusion is true. The premises are the statements the author uses to provide reasons for thinking the conclusion is true. If the argument is a good one, then the truth of the premises will give you good reasons for believing that the conclusion is true. If the argument is a bad one, then it will not give you reason to believe the truth of the conclusion. Thus, when you think about an argument, you need to ask yourself: What is the author trying to convince me of? What position is he trying to defend? This is the conclusion. The rest of the essay explains the connections between the premises and the conclusion, in order to establish why the premises are true and possibly to give examples to show that the argument is valid or strong.

There are two kinds of arguments: deductive and inductive. A **deductive argument** is one in which, if the argument is a good one, the premises guarantee the truth of the conclusion. For example, the following is a deductive argument:

(P1—premise 1) All dogs are animals.

(P2—premise 2) Ralph is a dog.

Therefore, (C—conclusion) Ralph is an animal.

Notice that if the first two statements are true (that is, that Ralph really is a dog and is not a cat or a fish or something else, and if, in fact, all dogs really are animals), then it must be the case that Ralph is an animal. The conclusion "Ralph is an animal" cannot be false if the premises are true.

In a good **inductive argument**, on the other hand, the truth of the premises only makes it *probable* that the conclusion is true. For example:

(P1) Most medical doctors are wealthy.

(P2) Dr. Gonzalez is a medical doctor.

Therefore, (C) Dr. Gonzalez is probably wealthy.

Notice that even if the premises are true—most doctors are wealthy and Dr. Gonzalez *is* a medical doctor—it still might not be true that Dr. Gonzalez is wealthy. P1 only claims that *most* doctors are wealthy, implying that some doctors are not. And Dr. Gonzalez may be one of the few who is not wealthy. So while we can be reasonably sure that Dr. Gonzalez is wealthy, we can't be absolutely positive in the same way we were absolutely positive that Ralph was an animal in the last example.

It is important that you understand the difference between deductive and inductive arguments, not only so that you can recognize them when you see them, but also so that you don't make the mistake of claiming that you have proven more than you really have. If an argument is inductive, then the best that can be said is that the conclusion is probably true. If you, or any other author, claim to have certainly proven your conclusion, the argument had better be deductive.

Of course, not all deductive or inductive arguments are good arguments. The two previous examples are good examples, but others aren't. There are two ways an argument can go "bad." First, *one or more of the premises may not be true*. In the first example above, if Ralph is something else and not a dog, then we can't be sure that he is an animal. (Maybe Ralph is my car.) Second, an argument can go wrong if something is wrong with its structure or form. For instance, consider the following argument:

(P1) If fetuses are people, then it is wrong to kill them.

(P2) Fetuses are not people.

Therefore, (C) it is not wrong to kill fetuses.

What's wrong with this argument? At first sight, maybe nothing. However, consider the following argument, which structurally is exactly the same:

(P1) If Ralph is a dog, then Ralph is an animal.

(P2) Ralph is not a dog.

Therefore, (C) Ralph is not an animal.

It is possible for both P1 and P2 to be true, but for C to be false. How? What if Ralph is a fish? P2 is true, since Ralph is not a dog. P1 is also true. Since all dogs are animals, then if Ralph was a dog, he would also be an animal. But it is not true that (C) Ralph is not an animal—fish are animals too! Since a good deductive argument is one in which the truth of the premises is supposed to guarantee the truth of the conclusion, this is not a good deductive argument. In fact, it is what we call an **invalid** argument. Validity has to do with the structure of the argument, not the content of the statements. What is wrong with these two arguments is not that any or all of the statements are false. What is wrong is that the conclusions don't follow from the premises. If the true premises in the argument about Ralph do not guarantee the truth of the conclusion, then even if the premises in the fetus argument are true, you can't be sure the conclusion is true—no matter how convincing you may have found it at first.

If an argument is **valid** and it has true premises, then it is called a **sound** argument. When I spoke of "good" arguments, these are the kind I meant—the premises are true, the form is valid, and thus we are guaranteed that the conclusion is also true. Trying to explain how to distinguish valid from invalid arguments is well beyond the scope of this book (see Appendix B for a list of books that address these issues). However, just being aware of the necessity of having both a valid argument and true premises will put you way ahead of the game.

Good inductive arguments are very similar to good deductive arguments. An inductive argument, remember, is one in which, if the premises are true, then the conclusion is probably true. Suppose I present the following argument:

(P1) Most professors are rich.

(P2) Dr. Gildrie is a professor.

Therefore (C) Dr. Gildrie is probably rich.

This is what we call a **strong** inductive argument. *If* the premises are true, then the conclusion is also probably true. However, this argument suffers from a false premise. In fact, it isn't true that most professors are rich.

Like a deductive argument, an inductive argument may have true premises but still not be a good argument. For example:

(P) I talked to 3 of my 126 students, and every one said I was the best teacher at the school.

Therefore, (C) I must be the best teacher at the school.

Notice that I talked to only 3 out of 126 students. That probably isn't very good evidence that I am the best teacher at the school. The premises in an inductive argument are supposed to give me good reasons for thinking the conclusion is probably true, and that just isn't the case here. Perhaps if I talked to 100 of the 126 students, or even 80 or 90 of them, then I might have a better reason for thinking I am the best teacher at the school. However, the fact that 3 students think I'm wonderful doesn't imply that they *all* do. This is what we call a **weak** inductive argument. The premises don't provide the necessary support for the conclusion. A good inductive argument—one in which not only are the premises true, but they also provide adequate support for thinking the conclusion is true—is called a **cogent** argument.

Again, teaching you everything you need to know in order to identify cogent arguments is beyond the scope of this book, but just be aware that, like deductive arguments, inductive arguments can have false premises or a weak form or both. But notice that just because an argument has one of these flaws, it isn't necessarily true that it has both flaws. Remember this example:

(P1) All dogs are animals.

(P2) Ralph is a dog.

Therefore, (C) Ralph is an animal.

If Ralph is a fish, then P2 is false, but the conclusion is true. Similarly, in the following example:

(P1) All dogs are animals.

(P2) Ralph is not a dog.

Therefore, (C) Ralph is not an animal.

If Ralph is my car, then the premises and the conclusion are true, but the argument has an invalid form and thus is not a good argument.

The moral of all this is that when you want to analyze an argument, you need to consider two things. First, if all the premises were true, would they give you good reason to think that the conclusion is true? Second, are all the premises true? To answer the first question, you either need to take a logic course or try to manage with the information I have given you here. In the second case, you need to consult the appropriate factual material. That is, in order to know if the premises of the previous argument are true, you need to (1) find out if all dogs are animals by consulting a biology book, your own memory, or your own common sense, and (2) take a look at Ralph to see if he is a dog or not.

ANALYZING ARGUMENTS

When you approach an argument or theory in order to analyze it, you must follow some very simple steps.

Identify the Main Conclusion

Each essay you read is probably trying to establish and convince you of one thing and one thing only. Ask yourself, What is the author's main point? He may have several secondary points, but the one main point should be pretty clear. (In fact, it is sometimes indicated in the title of the essay.) Probably it will be indicated in the first paragraph or two of the essay.

Identify the Premises

What supporting reasons does the author present for thinking his main point is true? Sometimes an author has hidden assumptions that may or may not be obvious to you. For example, if I say:

(P1) Ralph is a dog;

Therefore, (C) Ralph is an animal,

I have a hidden assumption (that all dogs are animals) and I am just assuming that you already know that. Some of these hidden assumptions—or unstated premises—will be common knowledge. However, some will not. You need to be sure that you make explicit anything that the author is assuming to be true that is crucial to his argument.

For example, suppose the author says:

(P1) The Bible says abortion is wrong.

Therefore, (C) abortion is wrong.

There are several unstated premises here. First of all, the speaker is assuming that the Bible is the word of God and thus what it says is true. This assumption implies that God exists, which many people don't believe. Whether the argument is good or bad isn't my point here. My point is simply that understanding this argument requires that you discover any unstated premises it relies on.

Clarify Any Ambiguous Words or Phrases

Authors often use words in a more technical way than they are used in common speech. So, for instance, an author who discusses "democracy" may not mean what you think she means. Clarifying the meaning of an author's terms may involve consulting a specialized political science dictionary or encyclopedia (see Appendix B). In any case, if you are not clear about what her words mean, you can never hope to be clear about what her argument means. At this point, you need to determine if the premises are true. You can't do that if you don't understand the words used in them.

Determine the Structure or Form of the Argument

Is the argument deductive or inductive? How do the premises fit together with the conclusion in order to prove the conclusion is true? Does the argument seem to be valid or strong? At this point, you need to give the author every benefit of the doubt that you can. That is, when you reconstruct his argument, add any assumptions needed to make it work, and put it into the best form possible. If on one reading of the argument it is obviously wrong and on another it is at least plausible, assume the second reading is the more accurate one. Determining its structure is the hardest part of analyzing an argument. Later in the chapter I will give you examples to show how this is done.

Watch for Emotional Language

Many people rely on **emotional language** in order to persuade you not to look too carefully at their arguments. Watch out for name calling, stereotypes, inflammatory language, and impassioned rhetoric that try to persuade you to adopt a conclusion for which sufficient proof has not been offered. Emotionally charged language is often used to persuade and convince the reader to accept a conclusion, without the arguer having to provide actual reasons or evidence to support that conclusion.

Check To See If There Are Any Fallacies Involved

A **fallacy** is a mistake made in an argument that *seems* correct but really isn't, often because of ambiguities in grammar or the meanings of words or because our inclination is to be convinced by reasons that are not good reasons. The fetus argument I gave earlier committed a formal fallacy. **Formal fallacies** have to do with the form or structure of the argument. An **informal fallacy** occurs when the form of the argument is valid or strong and the premises seem to be true, but the conclusion is (sometimes obviously) false, demonstrating that something has gone wrong in the argument. Checking for fallacies is so important that I will discuss it at length.

The False Dilemma Fallacy An author is guilty of a **false dilemma fallacy** when he draws a conclusion based on only two alternatives but there are other possibilities. Any time an author claims that there are only two alternatives, be very sure that there really *are* only two alternatives. If there is at least one more possibility, then the author has probably committed the false dilemma fallacy.

Consider the following passage from Plato's *Apology*. In this passage, Socrates is trying to explain to the Athenian jury why their sentencing him to death is not a bad thing:

> Let us reflect in another way, and we shall see that there is great reason to hope that death is a good, for one of two things: either death is a state of nothingness and utter unconsciousness, or, as men say, there is a change and migration of the soul from this world to another. Now if you suppose that there is no consciousness, but a sleep like the sleep of him who is undisturbed even by the sight of dreams, death will be an unspeakable gain. For if a person were to select the night in which his sleep was undisturbed even by dreams, and were to compare with this the other days and nights of his life, and then were to tell us how many days and nights he had passed in the course of his life better and more pleasantly than this one, I think that any man, I will not say a private man, but even the great

king [of Persia], will not find many such days or nights, when compared with the others. Now if death is like this, I say that to die is gain; for eternity is then only a single night. But if death is the journey to another place, and there, as men say, all the dead are, what good, O my friends and judges, can be greater than this? If indeed when the pilgrim arrives in the world below, he is delivered from the professors of justice in this world, and finds the true judges who are said to give judgment there, Minos and Rhadamanthus and Aeacus and Triptolemus, and other sons of God who were righteous in their own life, that pilgrimage will be worth making. What would not a man give if he might converse with Orpheus and Musaeus and Hesiod and Homer? Nay, if this be true, let me die again and again. I, too, shall have a wonderful interest in a place where I can converse with Palamedes, and Ajax the son of Telamon, and other heroes of old, who have suffered death through an unjust judgment; and there will be no small pleasure, as I think, in comparing my own sufferings with theirs. Above all, I shall be able to continue my search into true and false knowledge; as in this world, so also in that; I shall find out who is wise, and who pretends to be wise, and is not. What would not a man give, O judges, to be able to examine the leader of the great Trojan expedition; or Odysseus or Sisyphus, or numberless others, men and women too! What infinite delight would there be in conversing with them and asking them questions! For in that world they do not put a man to death for this; certainly not. For besides being happier in that world than in this, they will be immortal, if what is said is true.[1]

Socrates has committed the false dilemma fallacy. His argument looks like this:

(P1) Either death is nothing (like falling asleep and never waking up), or else death is going on to a better place.

(P2) If death is nothing, then there is no reason to fear it.

(P3) If death is going on to a better place, then there is no reason to fear it.

Therefore, (C) there is no reason to fear death.

This argument is *valid*—that is, if all the premises are true, then the conclusion must also be true. However, the first premise is not true, because Socrates implies that there are only two options: Either death is nothing, or else it is going on to a better place. In fact, it is possible that

---

[1] Plato, *Apology*, trans. Benjamin Jowett, in *The Greek Classics: Volume Four* (New York: Vincent Parke and Company, 1909), pp. 123–25.

there is at least one more option—that death might be going on to a *worse* place (like the Judeo-Christian hell). If the third option is true, then death *is* something to fear, and thus Socrates's argument doesn't work. Remember, when an author commits a fallacy, it indicates that something is wrong with his argument, and thus you have no assurance that his conclusion is true.

The Appeal to Unqualified Authority Fallacy Another common fallacy (which you are less likely to find in the essays you read for class than you are in your own essays) is the fallacy of **appeal to unqualified authority**. An appeal to authority occurs when you say, Such-and-such is true, because so-and-so said it. This can be legitimate in certain contexts. For example, if an argument depends upon a fact about astronomy, saying that Carl Sagan said it is true is probably justified. In the same way, if a premise makes a particular claim about when the fetus develops its central nervous system, then appealing to a respected child development expert or text is legitimate. On the other hand, an appeal to authority is only as good as the believability of the source. If your family doctor tells you that something is true about astronomy, you may not have good reason to believe that it is true. On the other hand, if Carl Sagan tells you that something is true about the development of the fetus, his saying so probably isn't a good reason to think it is true either. Thus people can be authorities in some areas but not in others. However, keep in mind that merely quoting an authority usually doesn't do any good. Just because John Locke claims something is true about democracy doesn't necessarily make it so—despite the fact that Locke is a famous, well-respected political philosopher. Questions in political science are often so complex and so uncertain that we don't usually consider anyone an authority. The *argument* is what is important, not what someone famous thought about the argument.

The False Cause Fallacy Another common fallacy is the fallacy of **false cause**. False cause involves claiming that one thing caused something else, when in fact it didn't. Sometimes the false cause is just something that happened at the same time. For example, consider the following argument:

(P1) Every time the cheerleaders wear blue ribbons in their hair, the football team wins.

(P2) We want the football team to win tonight's game.

Therefore, (C) the cheerleaders should wear blue ribbons in their hair tonight.

Obviously, the blue ribbons didn't *cause* the football team to win, but the argument implies that they did. Usually the problem is not that the supposed cause is not relevant to the effect, but that we claim it to be the only cause, when in fact it may be one of many. For example:

(P1) Teachers' salaries have been getting lower in terms of buying power every year for the past 10 years.

(P2) Students' SAT scores have been getting lower every year for the past 10 years.

Therefore, (C) if we raise teachers' salaries, then students will get higher scores on the SAT.

While it is possible that one reason students don't score well on the SAT is because their teachers are not well paid, it is not at all obvious (and probably isn't true) that teachers' low salaries are the sole cause of students' low scores.

The Is/Ought Fallacy   When an author claims that something ought to be the case simply because it is the case, he has committed one form of the **is/ought fallacy**. Some critics claim that John Stuart Mill commits this fallacy in his book *Utilitarianism*. Here are two passages to illustrate:

No reason can be given why the general happiness is desirable, except that each person, so far as he believes it to be attainable, desires his own happiness. . . .

If human nature is so constituted as to desire nothing which is not either a part of happiness or a means of happiness—we can have no other proof, and we require no other, that these are the only things desirable. If so, happiness is the sole end of human action, and the promotion of it the test by which to judge of all human conduct; from whence it necessarily follows that it must be the criterion of morality, since a part is included in the whole.[2]

In the first passage, Mill claims that everyone desires happiness (which is probably true). However, he goes on in the second passage to conclude that since everyone *does* desire happiness, they *ought* to desire happiness, and thus the creation of happiness should be what determines whether an action is moral or not. In other words, he claims that because something *is* the case, it *ought* to be the case. This is similar to arguing that since serial murderers enjoy killing people, then they *ought* to enjoy killing people. Or even, since serial murderers do kill people, it is mor-

---

[2] John Stuart Mill, *Utilitarianism*, Chapter IV, "Of What Sort of Proof the Principle of Utility Is Susceptible" (London: Parker, Son and Bourn, 1863).

ally right to kill people. We cannot, of course, make that connection. In this same context, Mill argues that

> the only proof capable of being given that an object is visible is that people actually see it. The only proof that a sound is audible is that people hear it. . . . In like manner, I apprehend, the sole evidence it is possible to produce that anything is desirable is that people do actually desire it.[3]

But Mill seems to be making a mistake here about the different meanings we attach to the words visible and desirable. By visible we just mean that people can see it, but by desirable we usually mean that people *should* desire it. Unless Mill makes the leap from "people do desire happiness" to "people should desire happiness," then his argument doesn't work. So Mill has committed the is/ought fallacy.

The Straw Man Fallacy   One of the hardest fallacies to detect is called the **straw man fallacy**. When an author commits the straw man fallacy, he changes the subject very subtly (from the "real man" to a "straw man" or irrelevant issue), so that he can attack it better. For example, if a person opposes prayer in the schools, she is often accused of being opposed to religion. This is a straw man because the issue is not religion as a whole, or even prayer in general, but only prayer in schools. An opposition to religion in general is easier to attack than the narrower issue of prayer in schools. Similarly, when the Equal Rights Amendment was being considered, one argument against it went like this:

> (P1) If the Equal Rights Amendment passes, then only unisex public toilets will be legal.

> (P2) Most people would be appalled to walk into a public toilet and find a person of the opposite sex in it.

> Therefore, (C) we should make sure the ERA doesn't pass.

This is a straw man argument. The point wasn't unisex toilets; the point was equal rights for women. Usually a person uses a straw man argument because he doesn't have very good reasons for opposing the original argument. So instead of knocking down the "real man" (the original argument), he erects a "straw man" and knocks it down instead, because a straw man is easier to topple.

---

[3] Mill, *Utilitarianism*, Chapter IV.

PUTTING IT ALL TOGETHER

If the argument form is valid or strong, the premises are all true, and the author has not committed any fallacies, then (and only then) can you be reasonably sure that the author's conclusion is correct. Unfortunately, authors do not always make this easy for you. Reconstructing an argument is hard work. Evaluating premises can be even harder. However, before you can have any hope of deciding whether you agree or disagree with an author's conclusion (which we'll discuss in Chapter 6), you need to be able to analyze his argument. Let's put it all together.

Consider the following passage from Chapter V of Mill's Utilitarianism:

> In our survey of the various popular acceptations of justice, the term appeared generally to involve the idea of a personal right—a claim on the part of one or more individuals, like that which the law gives when it confers a proprietary or other legal right. Whether the injustice consists in depriving a person of a possession, or in breaking faith with him, or in treating him worse than he deserves, or worse than other people who have no greater claims—in each case the supposition implies two things: a wrong done, and some assignable person who is wronged. . . . It seems to me that this feature in the case—a right in some person, correlative to the moral obligation—constitutes the specific difference between justice and generosity or beneficence. Justice implies something which is not only right to do, and wrong not to do, but which some individual person can claim from us as his moral right. No one has a moral right to our generosity or beneficence because we are not morally bound to practice those virtues toward any given individual. . . .
>
> When we call anything a person's right, we mean that he has a valid claim on society to protect him in the possession of it, either by the force of law or by that of education and opinion. If he has what we consider a sufficient claim, on whatever account, to have something guaranteed to him by society, we say that he has a right to it. If we desire to prove that anything does not belong to him by right, we think this is done as soon as it is admitted that society ought not to take measure for securing it to him, but should leave him to chance or to his own exertions. Thus a person is said to have a right to what he can earn in fair professional competition, because society ought not to allow any other person to hinder him from endeavoring to earn in that manner as much as he can. But he has not a right to three hundred a year, though he may happen to be earning it; because society is not called on to provide that he shall earn that sum. . . .

To have a right, then, is, I conceive, to have something which society ought to defend me in the possession of. If [an] objector goes on to ask why it ought, I can give him no other reason than general utility. If that expression does not seem to convey a sufficient feeling of the strength of the obligation, nor to account for the peculiar energy of the feeling, it is because there goes to the composition of the sentiment, not a rational only but also an animal element—the thirst for retaliation; and this thirst derives its intensity, as well as its moral justification, from the extraordinarily important and impressive kind of utility which is concerned. . . .

It appears from what has been said that justice is a name for certain moral requirements which, regarded collectively, stand higher in the scale of social utility, and are therefore of more paramount obligation, than any others, though particular cases may occur in which some other social duty is so important as to overrule any one of the general maxims of justice. Thus, to save a life, it may not only be allowable, but a duty, to steal or take by force the necessary food or medicine, or to kidnap and compel to officiate the only qualified medical practitioner. In such cases, as we do not call anything justice which is not a virtue, we usually say, not that justice must give way to some other moral principle, but that what is just in ordinary cases is, by reason of that other principle, not just in the particular case. . . .

Justice remains the appropriate name for certain social utilities which are vastly more important, and therefore more absolute and imperative, than any others are as a class (though not more so than others may be in particular cases); and which, therefore, ought to be, as well as naturally are, guarded by a sentiment, not only different in degree, but also in kind; distinguished from the milder feeling which attaches to the mere idea of promoting human pleasure or convenience at once by the more definite nature of its commands and by the sterner character of its sanctions.[4]

Now consider the following question:

What is Mill's argument regarding the connection between justice and utility?

Let's go through it following the five steps in analyzing an argument. First, the *conclusion* of this argument is that "Justice is simply the name for certain kinds of moral requirements which we consider most important on the scale of social utility." Second, the *premises* of the argument are as follows:

---

[4] Mill, *Utilitarianism*, Chapter V, "Of the Connection Between Justice and Utility."

(P1) Justice implies something that it would be right to do and wrong not to do.

(P2) Justice involves a moral right on the part of an individual, which should be protected by society.

(P3) The reason society should protect this moral right is because we feel that protecting these moral rights creates an "extraordinarily important and impressive kind" of happiness (social utility) which we consider much more important than other kinds of happiness.

Third, *are there any words whose meanings need to be clarified*? Aside from his use of "social utility" and "the expedient" as synonyms for the general happiness, no. *Are there any hidden assumptions*? Only the principle of utility (that what makes actions right is that they lead to happiness), which isn't really hidden since this chapter follows his arguments defending that principle. *Are all his premises true?* That is debatable. In (P3) Mill claims that protecting our moral rights leads to a most important kind of happiness. Is that true? That is, are we really happier when people are treated fairly, when they are allowed to keep what they already own, and when like cases are treated alike? Sometimes, surely we are. But at least sometimes, it seems to me, we aren't. Of course, Mill responds to that by saying that in those cases, we don't want what is unjust, but some stronger principle overrides them, and thus that stronger principle is what is just. Fourth, *what is the structure of the argument*? It is probably meant to be deductive. That is, Mill seems to suggest that given the premises about what justice is and how we feel about it, it follows that "justice" is simply the name of certain actions that usually create more happiness than any of the alternatives. Fifth, does Mill *commit any fallacies or use any emotive language*? Probably not, unless you count the is/ought fallacy he commits in defending the original principle of utility. Is this a good argument? If you accept the principle of utility as a given, then this argument is probably a good one. Now you are ready to write your analysis. (I'll leave it to your imagination!)

6

WRITING FOR EVALUATION

The **evaluative essay** (or as it is sometimes called, **the argumentative essay**) is probably the most common essay required of students. In an evaluative essay, you are asked to criticize or defend something you've read, usually an argument, theory, or essay. You are asked to make a judgment about whether the argument is a good or bad argument, whether the author is right or wrong, and whether you agree or disagree with him. However, if you just say that the author is right, that he has a good argument, and that you agree with him, all you have done is express your opinion. In an evaluative essay, your opinion must be supported by reliable evidence and strong reasoning. That is, you must provide an argument for why your interpretation of the author's argument or idea is the correct one.

Being critical of an argument does not mean being hostile to or intolerant of it. What it does mean is that you carefully consider the author's premises and conclusion and make a judgment about whether those premises are true, whether they provide relevant support for her conclusion, whether her examples and analogies are appropriate, whether she commits any fallacies, and so on. If you have not read Chapter 5, go back and do so now. You cannot write an evaluative essay without first being able to analyze the argument you are evaluating.

CHOOSING/DEVELOPING A THESIS

If your instructor allows you to choose your own topic (that is, what theory or essay you want to evaluate), think small. Trying to cover "What's wrong with Locke's political theory" in three to five pages is impossible. Of course, the longer the paper is supposed to be, the broader your thesis should be. At the introductory level, theses are generally broader than in more advanced classes. The less you know, the less you have to say about a subject, and the more you know, the more you can say. It is, of course, possible to think too small. If you find that you have said everything you know in one page, you need to broaden your thesis. However, if the topic was assigned by your instructor, then the fact that you can only write one page is an indication that you aren't thinking deeply or thoroughly enough.

As we saw in Chapter 5, there are two general ways to criticize an argument. The first is to *assess the structure of the argument*—is it valid or invalid, strong or weak? Do the premises provide relevant and sufficient evidence for thinking the conclusion is true? In fact, many arguments that you read probably will not be deductively invalid or inductively weak. Thus, the second way to criticize an argument is to *criticize the content of the argument*. Are the premises true? Does the author **equivocate** about the meaning of his terms? Does he commit any informal fallacies? Once you have answered these questions to your own satisfaction, you need to formulate your **thesis**—your opinion regarding what is wrong (or right) with the argument.

THE EVALUATIVE ESSAY

The evaluative essay usually follows a particular pattern. The beginning of the essay, the introduction, should include not only a full statement of whether you agree or disagree with the author, but also a preliminary statement of your reasons for why you agree or disagree. Of course, until you analyze the argument, you won't know whether (and why) you agree or disagree. Thus, writing your introduction will be one of the last things you do.

In the body of the essay, you will need to state the author's argument precisely, completely, and in a detailed way. You need to analyze the argument, as we did in Chapter 5, by carefully identifying both the premises and the structure of the argument. Then you should critically evaluate the argument. In doing so, you need to make it clear what you object to, give your reasons for why you object, show that you have thought about how the author might respond to your objection, and consider how seriously your objection damages the argument.

Finally, in your conclusion, you should provide a brief summary and review of your argument, and perhaps give an indication of any further implications it might have. Typically, your conclusion will be fairly brief and should not be too repetitive.

EXAMPLE: LOCKE'S THEORY OF PROPERTY

Say you have been assigned or have chosen to argue against John Locke's theory of property. First, consider the following passage from Locke:

> Whether we consider natural reason, which tells us, that men, being once born, have a right to their preservation, and consequently to meat and drink, and such other things as nature affords for their subsistence. . . . But this being supposed, it seems to some a very great difficulty, how any one should ever come to have a property in any thing. . . . I shall endeavour to shew, how men might come to have a property in several parts of that which God gave to mankind in common, and that without any express compact of all the commoners. . . .
>
> Though the earth, and all inferior creatures, be common to all men, yet every man has a property in his own person: this no body has any right to but himself. The labour of his body, and the work of his hands, we may say, are properly his. Whatsoever then he removes out of the state that nature hath provided, and left it in, he hath mixed his labour with, and joined to it something that is his own, and thereby makes it his property. It being by him removed from the common state nature hath placed it in, it hath by this labour something annexed to it, that excludes the common right of other men: for this labour being the unquestionable property of the labourer, no man but he can have a right to what that is once joined to, at least where there is enough, and as good, left in common for others.
>
> He that is nourished by the acorns he picked up under an oak, or the apples he gathered from the trees in the wood, has certainly appropriated them to himself. No body can deny but the nourishment is his. I ask then, when did they begin to be his? when he digested? or when he eat? or when he boiled? or when he brought them home? or when he picked them up? and it is plain, if the first gathering made them not his, nothing else could. That labour put a distinction between them and common: that added something to them more than nature, the common mother of all, had done; and so they be-

came his private right. . . . We see in commons, which remain so by compact, that it is the taking any part of what is common, and removing it out of the state nature leaves it in, which begins the property; without which the common is of no use. And the taking of this or that part, does not depend on the express consent of all the commoners. Thus the grass my horse has bit; the turfs my servant has cut; and the ore I have digged in any place, where I have a right to them in common with others, become my property, without the assignation or consent of any body. The labour that was mine, removing them out of that common state they were in, hath fixed my property in them. . . .

It will perhaps be objected to this, that if gathering the acorns, or other fruits of the earth, &c. makes a right to them, then any one may ingross as much as he will. To which I answer, Not so. The same law of nature, that does by this means give us property, does also bound that property too. . . . As much as any one can make use of to any advantage of life before it spoils, so much he may by his labour fix a property in: whatever is beyond this, is more than his share, and belongs to others. Nothing was made by God for man to spoil or destroy. . . .

But the chief matter of property being now not the fruits of the earth, and the beasts that subsist on it, but the earth itself; as that which takes in and carries with it all the rest; I think it is plain, that property in that too is acquired as the former. As much land as a man tills, plants, improves, cultivates, and can use the product of, so much is his property.[1]

Summarize Locke's Argument

An ideal way to start your evaluative essay on Locke's property argument would be to write a brief summary (see Chapter 3) of his argument. Notice that in the summary below, I also provide examples and specifics to make the various points clear.

According to Locke, the earth and all it's creatures were given to people in common for nourishment and life. That being the case, no one owned anything privately—not land, animals, or plants. The only thing people have an absolute right to ownership in is themselves—their bodies, and the labor of their bodies. Locke says that since people own the labor of their bodies, then when they mix that

---

[1] John Locke, *The Second Treatise of Government: An Essay Concerning the Origin, Extent and End of Civil Government*, Chapter V, "Of Property" (1690).

labor with common property, they acquire ownership in that property. For example, if I pick the apples, the apples become mine. If I plow and plant and reap the crops from a piece of land, then that land becomes my own. However, Locke also says that I can't acquire property in any more than I can make use of before it spoils. So if I spend all day picking apples, they don't all become mine if most of them will rot before I use them.

Analyze the Argument

The next thing you need to do is analyze that argument, as you learned to do in Chapter 5. First, outline Locke's premises and conclusions:

(P1):   All of creation was given to people in common for life and nourishment.

(P2):   Each person owns her own body and the labor of her body.

(C):   Thus, property is acquired by "mixing our labor with" commonly held objects and land.

This is the main structure of Locke's argument. Notice that Locke's argument is probably intended to be a deductive argument. That is, if his premises are true, then he claims that his conclusion must be true.

Describe Your Position

The next step is to write a description of your own position, summarizing your own argument briefly. For example:

I intend to argue that Locke is wrong about how we acquire property—or at least, he is wrong about how we acquire property in this day and age.

Once you have analyzed the argument, you will have discovered any weak points—false or doubtful premises, informal fallacies, premises that don't support the conclusion, and so on. Now is the time to do some hard thinking about how successful you find the argument. Does it work? Are there problems? Has the author claimed to prove more than he has proved? What do you agree or disagree with and why? Must his conclusion be rejected completely or can his premises provide support for a different, perhaps more restricted, conclusion?

There are several things to keep in mind as you prepare your evaluation. A bad argument for a conclusion does not prove that the conclusion is false. All it proves is that it's a bad argument—that is, that these premises do not provide good evidence for the conclusion. So be sure you don't conclude that since Locke's argument doesn't work, that proves that no one should own private property. Keep in mind also that your instructor is not as interested in what you *think* about Locke's argument, but in the reasons and arguments that you provide for *why* you think it. Now flesh out your earlier statement of your position:

> I think Locke is wrong about how we acquire property in land and things. In the first place, if something is truly held in common—that is, it belongs to everyone—then simply picking the apples doesn't make them mine. Of course, Locke says that there's plenty to go around, so even if I pick a bunch of apples, there are plenty left for others, but clearly that is not true today. My second objection to Locke's theory comes when he says that a person can "own" only what she can use before it spoils. Unless he means that I can sell my excess, then this would prohibit any accumulation of wealth or things at all. Even if neither of the previous objections are fatal to his theory, I think that he is still wrong about how we acquire property. His theory would justify the way the early Americans "appropriated" the Indians' land for their own use. The settlers put their labor into the land by plowing it and fencing it, so the Indians were basically out of luck.

Outline Your Essay

Now, put everything together into an outline. An outline provides structure for your essay, helping you to organize your thoughts and to spot any weak points in your argument. It also insures that you don't get side-tracked from the main issue. The outline can help you recognize problems with the structure of your argument, as well as any possible weak points. When you begin with an outline, you establish control over your essay. Of course, it is entirely possible that as you write you will begin to deviate from the original outline. This is perfectly natural and sometimes useful. I began each chapter of this book with a *very* rough outline, but very few chapters ended up exactly following the outline. Your outline isn't written in stone. It is not supposed to restrict and confine you in any way. It is simply a tool to make your writing easier and to improve the final product. It insures that when you begin writing, you already have a clear idea of where you want to go. Here is a sample outline for an argument written in response to the Locke essay:

I. Introduction:

    A. Define property held in common.

    B. Explain how Locke says we acquire property.

    C. (Thesis Statement) Locke's argument about how we acquire property doesn't work, or, at least, it is irrelevant today.

II. Locke's argument:

   A. All of creation was given to people in common for life and nourishment.

   B. Each person owns her own body and the labor of her body.

   C. Thus, property is acquired by "mixing our labor with" commonly held objects and land.

III. Critique of Locke's argument:

   A. If something is truly held in common—that is, it belongs to everyone—then simply picking the apples doesn't make them mine. Of course, Locke says that there's plenty to go around, so even if I pick a bunch of apples, there are plenty left for others, but clearly that is not true today.

   B. He says that a person can "own" only what she can use before it spoils. Unless he means that I can sell my excess, then this would prohibit any accumulation of wealth or things at all.

   C. His theory would justify the way the early Americans "appropriated" the Indians's land for their own use.

   D. Since land is no longer "held in common", his theory is irrelevant to today's society.

IV. How Locke might reply:

Locke would argue that there is no other way that we can acquire property than the way he presented. Thus, if we can't acquire property his way, we can't legitimately acquire property at all.

V. Conclusion

Locke's argument does not show how we legitimately acquire property. In particular, I think that since his argument doesn't work, that private ownership of property is not legitimate.

Notice that I wrote this outline with complete sentences (mostly) and I made it as comprehensive as possible. The outline runs to several pages all by itself. Writing an essay from it should prove relatively easy. I've already made most of my points in the outline. To write the essay, all I have to do is put these ideas into coherent sentences and paragraphs with the appropriate connecting words and thoughts. In fact, most of the hard work has been done by the time I finish the outline.

Write the Essay

Just because I wrote a very complete and comprehensive outline doesn't mean that I won't change my mind as I begin to write the paper. I have to flesh out my ideas and objections to the argument, and as I do so, I may realize that some of my points aren't as strong as I thought, that I have misinterpreted something Aristotle said or that there is a more sympathetic way to interpret what he said, or that there are other, better objections to his argument than the ones I initially came up with. Your outline is not sacred—change it at will. Just be sure that you wind up with an organized essay. If you change your outline, then when you finish writing your essay, re-outline it to be sure that the structure is still clear. If the essay wanders off on tangents, re-outlining will help you recognize the problems.

CONCLUDING REMARKS

Don't forget the principle of charity mentioned in Chapter 2. The author found his argument particularly compelling—or else he wouldn't have written it. Put yourself into his shoes and try to figure out why a rational, well-meaning person would accept the premises and conclusion. Your evaluation should be appropriate and fair, your tone should be respectful throughout the essay, and you should avoid committing fallacies or using emotive language. Despite the fact that you disagree with the author's conclusion and/or his argument, you should not be intolerant, abusive, or malicious in your criticism.

Evaluating someone else's argument is good practice before you try to create your own arguments, which we will discuss in the next chapter. In discovering and criticizing common mistakes, you can give yourself a jump start on avoiding them in your own writing. It is much easier to criticize someone else's argument than it is to come up with a new and original argument of your own. As you may already have discovered in your reading, much scholarly writing consists of one author discussing and evaluating the arguments of an earlier author. Any idea, argument, or theory is fair game. A theory worth holding is a theory worth criticizing. If it can't stand up to critical evaluation, then it isn't worth believing in the first place.

SAMPLE ESSAY

This essay was written by a junior history major in a lower-division course on Ethics. It is not perfect, of course. However, she does a reasonably good job of analyzing and evaluating the original essay.

Mill's Views on Free Speech

Tami Bays

In John Stuart Mill's article "Of Liberty of Thought and Discussion," he examines the right of free speech. Mill believed that preserving the right of free speech is of vital social significance. He states that there is no reason to prohibit free speech because to limit speech is to limit humankind's knowledge of the truth. Mill utilizes three arguments concerning free speech and truth and one argument concerning liberty to support his views. I believe that in most circumstances free speech should be preserved. However, there are clear instances in which it would not be beneficial to do so.

The first argument Mill presents is that if an opinion is silenced, that opinion may be true and the opportunity to hear the truth is thereby denied. The person who does not hear the truth is unable to exchange or modify his/her false opinion for the accurate one. Mill thinks that this is a grievous error because one of humankind's chief concerns is discovering the truth. Mill even goes so far to say that stifling an opinion is evil. Mill denies that one can ever know what truth really is. Humans are fallible and one can never be sure that his/her own opinion is true. To refuse to allow an opposing opinion to be heard is to say that one is certain that one's own opinion is true and the other is false. If I deny someone the ability to speak his/her opinion, I am essentially saying that he/she is wrong. Mill says that I cannot know the other person is wrong until I hear his/her opinion. This also allows one to reinforce one's own opinion. By hearing the other side, one can strengthen one's own argument and gain rational assurance of one's own rightness.

The second argument Mill utilizes is that if an opinion goes unopposed, it will lose its meaning. Mill calls an argument that is not discussed a "dead dogma" and one that is openly communicated a "living truth." He believes that an idea kept alive by discussion is better understood overall. One must be "equally able to refute the reasons on the opposite side" in order to strengthen one's own argument. Mill also says that it is important for people to hear opinions from people who honestly believe in them. This honesty will lead to better understanding for all parties involved.

The third reason Mill states in his argument that free speech preserves truth is that truth may be found between many arguments. One opinion may contain pieces of truth, while missing the whole truth. By combining many different views, a better understanding of the whole truth may be obtained. Opposition from another may provide the remainder of the truth. Many arguments may contain part of the truth. Mill says that "every opinion which embodies somewhat of a portion of truth which the common opinion omits ought to be considered precious."

Mill is also concerned about liberty when he is considering free speech. He says that it is as unjust to silence one individual as it is to silence mankind as a whole. It is also impeding liberty to deny the truth. He asserts that "complete liberty of contradicting and disproving opinion is the very condition which justifies us in assuming its truth." Mill states that those who oppose this belief feel that it is the duty of governments and individuals to form opinions carefully and not impose them onto others "unless they are quite sure of being right." If humans are fallible and can never be sure they are right, then this implies that one should never express his/her opinion to others. However, this is clearly not what Mill wants us to do and he disagrees strongly with the aforementioned opposing argument.

I support Mill's principle; however, there are some cases in which free speech is clearly harmful. I agree that free speech and freedom of expression are values fundamental to our liberty. Mill assumes that all speech is more beneficial than harmful. He does not express any limits on free speech and I cannot agree that freedom of expression should be unlimited. I think it is clear that child pornography is not a beneficial form of free expression. To accept no limits on free speech would be to accept certain things that would lead to more harm than benefit. For example, in 1999, a pro-life web site was posting the names of doctors working at abortion clinics all over the United States. When one of the listed clinics was bombed, a line was drawn through the corresponding doctor's name. It is apparent that this encouraged extreme and violent pro-lifers to seek out doctors on the list for attack. Overall this was extremely harmful for those who appeared on the list. Mill would probably have a hard time knowing where to draw the line when it comes to hate speech, as most of us do today. When does free speech become truly harmful and how can one determine when liberty is infringed in a way that is not beneficial for the whole? This is a question Mill does not address in his essay.

In Mill's essay "Of the Liberty of Thought and Discussion", he makes a claim that free speech should be preserved in order to promote truth and liberty. I agree that by sharing our opinions with others, we can discover our own mistakes and have the opportunity to correct them. Prohibiting free speech and freedom of expression infringes on humankind's basic right to liberty. However, in some instances, such as child pornography, free speech should be limited for the good of the community. I feel that Mill failed to place limitations on free speech in his article and thereby ignored the harm free speech is capable of inflicting.

References: John Stuart Mill, *On Liberty*, Chapter II, "Of the Liberty of Thought and Discussion" (London: Longman, Roberts & Green, 1869)

7

WRITING FOR SYNTHESIS

A **synthesis essay** is primarily a **thesis defense paper**: That is, you take a position on an issue and then defend it. It involves bringing together elements of several different arguments to create a new whole. You will rarely be asked to write a synthesis essay on an in-class exam—usually it will be assigned as a longer, out-of-class essay. However, a synthesis essay is not a research paper that merely reports what other people have said. Nor is it simply an expression of your feelings or emotions. It is not simply a collection of stories or examples. And it is not a compilation of quotations from a number of different sources. A synthesis essay is, at its most basic, an attempt to persuade someone of something. As with evaluative essays, you must give reasons and present evidence for why your position is correct, and then you must defend your thesis against objections. You argue that there are much better reasons for accepting your thesis than there are for rejecting it, or much better reasons for accepting it than for accepting any of the alternatives.

Unlike the evaluative essay, however, your position will not represent an evaluation of someone else's theory; it will be an original position that you yourself believe and want to support. I use the term "original" loosely, of course. You may argue that capital punishment is justified, that abortion is not immoral, or that civil disobedience should not be tolerated, and, of course, plenty of people will have argued for these same conclusions before you. What will be original, with luck, will be—not your conclusion—but your argument proving that conclusion. Of

50

course, you can rarely hope to prove that your thesis is absolutely, positively true, but you should try to show why an ordinary, rational person should believe it. Unless you are extraordinarily innovative, you probably won't come up with a position that is completely original. Don't worry—your instructor doesn't expect it!

We all have presented our own arguments in favor of something at some time. When you try to convince your friends to go see the movie you want to see instead of an alternative, you present them with reasons and evidence for why your chosen movie is the better choice. When you try to convince your parents that you need a new car, or a guitar, or a tattoo, you use an argument to convince them. (And I don't, of course, mean an argument in the sense that you get angry and scream and yell. Once you do that, you have given up on the kind of argument I'm talking about.) An argumentative essay requires more care and depth than these kinds of arguments. The kind of evidence that may be persuasive in casual conversation is usually not acceptable in a political science class.

What is important in a thesis defense paper is not usually what position you argue for, but how you argue for it. Recall this example from Chapter 1:

> Which is the better form of government—direct democracy or representative democracy? Provide an argument to support your position.

Your instructor probably isn't concerned with which form of government you prefer, but you must decide which position you think is best, so that you can build your essay around that claim. This kind of essay may well be the most difficult one you ever write. Because of that, it is important that you choose your thesis well. *Choose a thesis that is worth arguing for.* Only when a conclusion is not obvious is it necessary to argue for it. If you choose a position so obvious that practically no one disagrees, or if you choose a controversial position on a trivial subject, you are wasting your time. If your instructor provides you with a choice (as in the example above), then you need only choose to argue one side or the other. It is, of course, much easier to argue for something you believe. On the other hand, be open to the possibility that as you write and accumulate evidence, you may decide to change your mind.

OUTLINE

It is very important that you create at least a rough outline before you begin writing. (See Chapter 6.) The structure of a synthesis essay is very simple:

I. Introduction: State your thesis (conclusion).
II. Give your reasons and supporting evidence (premises) for that conclusion.
III. Show not only that your premises are true, but that they prove the conclusion.
IV. Present objections to your position (counter-arguments).
V. Explain why each of those objections fail.
VI. Conclusion: Summarize and review what you have accomplished and what it means.

This is the most basic of outlines. Any synthesis essay you write will take this form or something very like it. The trick is to begin with this bare outline, and then add to it.

Suppose you want to argue that there is no moral right to property. Part I of your outline would read:

I. Introduction:
   It is not morally permissible to own private property.

In this first part of your essay you will briefly state how you plan to prove your thesis. You also may want to explain what the issue is and why you think it is important. You can put all of this in your outline if you want to. The more complete your outline is, the easier your essay will be to write.

Part II, then, should be your reasons for why you think your thesis is true. Refer back to the way we analyzed arguments in Chapter 5. You need to use these same steps in creating your own argument. Lay out each premise and the conclusion:

II. Argument:
   A. Equality is of primary concern in a democratic society.
   B. Allowing individuals to own private property inevitably results in an unequal distribution of material goods.
   C. Thus, people should not be allowed to own private property.

In Part III you will show why your premises should be accepted. In fact, you may need to provide an argument for one or more of your premises in order to show why it is true. In this case, you would probably need to provide an argument for premise A, particularly explaining why equality is more important than the freedom to do what you want (including owning private property.) Part III is not so easy to outline. To help you in your writing, you should probably at least indicate some of your reasons for thinking your premises are true. For example:

III. Truth of premises:
   A. While the freedom to do as we chose (including owning private property) is very important in a democratic society, equality is more important.
   B. Give reasons for why equality is more important than liberty.

Notice a couple of things in this outline. First, I have used complete sentences. This isn't strictly necessary, but it is a good habit to get into, since writing the essay will be much easier if you are starting with complete sentences. Second, in Part II, I reveal a particular bias I am taking in this essay—that is, I believe that equality is a value that overrides liberty. Although I will try to prove it in section III, if my sub-argument is not convincing, then my argument will not work.

In Part IV you will respond to objections to your position. This may involve responding to things some other author has actually said, or it may involve responding to possible objections. For example, John Locke has written at some length about the right to own property and the basis of that right. You should certainly explain his argument, and then give your own counter-argument which shows why Locke is wrong. So Part IV of your outline may look like this:

IV. Objections:
   A. Locke's argument for why we have a right to own property.

   B. Other author's objections to Marx's idea of abolishing private property.

In Part V you need to respond to those objections and explain why they fail to refute your argument. So, for example:

V. Response to objections:
   A. Locke is wrong to think that simply using my labor to produce something gives me the right to keep it for my own use.

   B. Response to others.

Note that while I have put all the objections in Part IV and all the responses in Part V, it would probably be better to write the essay this way:

IV. Objections and responses:
   A. Locke's argument for why we have a right to own property. Response: Locke is wrong to think that simply using my labor to produce something gives me the right to keep it for my own use.

Finally, Part VI is the conclusion of your essay (which, as we know, restates the conclusion of your argument). In addition, Part VI should indicate some of the consequences of accepting that conclusion. So,

VI. Conclusion:
    A. It is immoral for people to own private property.
    B. This means that:
       1. We will have to figure out a way to continually redistribute wealth so that individuals can't buy things.
       2. We will have to figure out a way to remove currently owned property from its owners and give it to the state.
       3. We may have to change the way we reward people for products and services.

Your Part VI may not be this detailed, but when I prepare an outline, I try to include all the important points I want to make so that I don't forget them!

If you begin with a very complete outline like this one, you will find writing your essay much easier. Even if you decide not to write an outline before you begin, you should certainly try to outline the essay after you finish writing it. If you do start with an outline and you depart from it, you should probably outline again after you finish. If, when your essay is completed, you can write a fairly coherent and intelligible outline, then you know that the essay itself is fairly coherent and intelligible. If, on the other hand, you cannot create a plausible outline, then you know that the essay has problems that must be fixed. Organizational and structural problems will be very clear in the outline. Of course, there may be other problems with the essay that the outline won't catch, but since coherence, clarity, and consistency are some of the most important elements in any essay, take my advice and write an outline!

EVIDENCE

Notice that my outline shows that I have reasons for why I believe my thesis is true. I do not simply say "I feel" or "I believe." Readers don't care how you *feel* about private property. Their feelings may not be the same as yours. In order to persuade them that your feelings are right, you have to provide an argument that consists of reasons why any rational, well-meaning person should also feel as you do. Don't mistake having an opinion for being right. A thesis that is not supported by reasons or evidence is not an argument. Your instructor is less interested in what you believe (your thesis) than she is in how well you argue for that thesis. When you do not provide reasons in support of your thesis, or when you provide weak or poorly supported reasons, you weaken your essay.

Use the strongest and most convincing reasons (premises) you can find to support your position. As I suggested, you may need to provide subarguments to show why your premises are true. Many of your premises will not need such support, but at least some of them probably will. Not only must your reasons be convincing, but you must also be sure that together they form a chain of reasoning that will allow your reader to arrive at the same conclusion you do. This means that your conclusion probably should not contradict common sense. If your conclusion is too far out in left field, you will lose your reader fairly quickly. At the same time, simply because your conclusion seems to contradict common sense is not necessarily a reason for not defending it. *If* you make your thesis as clear as possible, and *if* you make sure that every point in your essay supports that thesis, and *if* each of those supporting points is clear in itself, and *if* you can make it clear how the structure of the argument works—that is, how the premises fit together to establish the truth of the conclusion—then any possible thesis is fair game. Of course, all those *ifs* apply even if your thesis doesn't contradict common sense.

In providing evidence for your conclusion, do not rely solely on examples. An example usually is not enough to establish the truth of a point. But using examples *can* help to clarify points, illustrate the point being made, or suggest what is wrong with a counter-argument. Good examples can improve an essay dramatically, while bad or irrelevant examples really detract from the quality of an essay. Use examples wisely, but use them (see Chapter 4).

Notice that the kind of evidence offered in support of the thesis about private property was not scientific or religious in nature. Questions in political science can almost never be solved by appeals to science, religion, experience, personal feelings, psychology, or social causes. They cannot be resolved by appeals to authorities ("Locke said so" or "The Bible says so"). These kinds of questions can only be answered by the process of providing reasonable and relatively unambiguous reasons that fit together in an appropriate way so that they either establish the truth of the conclusion or at least make it more likely to be true than not.

You should also be careful not to claim to have proved more than you actually have. If you can only show that something is true in *most* cases, then don't claim that it is *always* true.

Remember the distinction made in Chapter 5 between deductive and inductive arguments? Often it is impossible to achieve the deductive standard of proving your thesis with certainty. If so, acknowledge the uncertainty and settle for less. If you can't prove beyond any doubt that owning private property is wrong, don't claim that you can. However, if you can show that there is a strong probability that owning private property is wrong, or that in most cases owning private property is wrong, or even that the evidence opposing owning private property seems to be stronger than the evidence in favor of it, then say so, and realize that this is quite an accomplishment in itself.

Students often think that evaluation simply consists of differences in opinion. It's just my opinion against your opinion, and because everyone's opinion is as good as anyone else's, there is no way to decide who is right. Many people think that anyone who believes something strongly enough and expresses himself loudly enough deserves to have his "argument" respected. This is not true in political science or in any other academic area. I tell my students that we don't traffic in opinions, we traffic in arguments. That is, while people do have different opinions, the way to decide who is right is to decide who presents the best argument—in the form of evidence, reasons, and proofs. Shouting your opinion isn't any better than whispering it. And simply because many people agree with your opinion is not grounds for thinking your opinion is right. Opinions must be supported by reasons. If they are not, then they *are* merely opinions, and they probably *are* equal. The moral of this story is that without reasons to support your thesis, your "argument" is relatively useless.

COUNTER-ARGUMENTS

In the basic outline, Parts IV and V involved presenting counter-arguments (or objections to your argument) and showing why the counter-arguments fail. Notice that in my outline for the essay on private property, I responded to several kinds of objections. Locke's objection had to do with a direct objection to my thesis, but not necessarily to the particular argument I presented in support of that thesis. Other counter-arguments might be objections to particular premises within my argument. Also notice that one objection (Locke's again) was an argument that someone actually used (and thus should be footnoted—see Chapter 8). The other objections may be just sort of generic objections that someone *could* use against my argument.

Your argument will be much stronger if you consider objections and counter-arguments. By showing that you are aware of the concerns of others, and by showing that your own argument can withstand their criticisms, you strengthen your position considerably. On the other hand, if you find you cannot adequately respond to their criticisms, then there is something wrong with your argument. However, don't fall into the trap of using weak counter-arguments that are certain to be unconvincing. Weak counter-arguments simply make your own argument weaker. If you find that you can't refute the counter-arguments, then you may need to consider changing your own thesis. You may decide to change sides completely (for example, argue that owning private property is morally justified), or you may decide simply to weaken your thesis (and argue that owning private property *probably* or *usually* isn't justified, or that owning *some* kinds of property isn't justified). Controversial issues are controversial simply because there are good, persuasive arguments on both sides, which well-meaning people of good faith accept.

While I presented several possible counter-arguments in my outline, unless you are writing a fairly lengthy essay, you probably will not need too many. Often you will choose your thesis on the basis of some essay with which you disagree. If so, use that essay as a counter-argument. In any case, it is very important that you keep your mind open enough about your thesis that you can understand and reconstruct the arguments of those who disagree with you. This means that you must try to fairly and accurately represent those positions with which you disagree. I could tell you that this practice is good for you and it builds character, but I'm not your mother. What I can tell you is that presenting and refuting counter-arguments contributes to a *much* better (translation: higher grade) essay than not doing so.

PUTTING IT ALL TOGETHER

The Introduction

When you begin to write your essay based on your outline, don't start with the introduction. I know that is counter-intuitive, but you should probably write your introduction last—or at least expect to come back to it after you have finished the rest of the essay and done some major revisions. The reason for writing the introduction last is that, even with a good outline, you will rarely be sure of exactly what you are going to argue and how you are going to argue for it. Your introduction needs not only to state your thesis, but also to summarize how you intend to prove that thesis, and you may not be able to describe that in any detail when you start out. Begin by writing the body of the paper. Start with your argument and its premises and the connections and inter-relationships between them.

When you do write your introduction, your thesis statement probably won't be the first sentence. You need to build up to it. What is the issue at hand? Why is it important? What is the context in which this issue is located? Don't start with a dictionary definition: "Webster's defines democracy as . . . ." Don't start with a huge generalization:

"Throughout history, people have been concerned about . . . ." Don't start with: "In this paper I will . . . ." Don't begin your essay with your first premise—at this early stage, your reader has no idea why it's relevant. Do begin by establishing your topic and discussing its importance, relevance, and perhaps timeliness. For example, in the essay on private property, you could begin by stating what exactly the issue is. What is private property? Why would anyone want to prohibit it? You might then go on to give some examples of the kind of problems that arise by allowing people to own private property.

By the end of your first, or maybe second, paragraph you should have stated your thesis, so that the reader has no doubt what position you plan to defend. By the end of your introduction, the reader should also have a reasonably clear idea about how you plan to prove that thesis. Your introduction should be so clear that even someone who knows nothing of democracy or Marxism (for example) can understand not only what the issue is, but also what your position on it is, and, in a general way, how you plan to go about persuading him that you are right.

Here is an example of a brief introduction for the essay on private property. Notice that if the essay were to be a very long one, the introduction would probably need to be longer as well.

> If we could shrink the earth's population to a village of precisely 100 people, with all the existing human ratios remaining the same, 6 people would possess 59% of the entire world's wealth and all 6 would be from the United States; 50 would suffer from malnutrition; 80 would live in substandard housing; and only 1 would own a computer. When individuals privately own land, resources, and products, they have the exclusive right to do with them as they choose. They can use it, sell it, destroy it, give it away, or let it sit idle. But their freedom to do so comes at the expense of many other people.
>
> Because equality is the primary overriding value in a democracy, I believe that private ownership of property is immoral. While liberty is an important value, and a democracy is based upon the respect for individual freedom, because of the gross imbalance of ownership illustrated in the previous paragraph, equality is more important than liberty. In this essay, I intend to argue that ownership of private property is immoral.

Notice that this introduction gives the context of the discussion (by explaining what the issue is), uses some striking examples to capture the reader's interest, and presents the thesis as well as indicates why the author thinks her thesis is true. Above all, your introduction needs to be interesting enough to make the reader want to read further. Yes, your instructor is going to read through to the end no matter how boring your introduction is, but he may not read it in quite the frame of mind you desire if he's been bored senseless by your introduction. Other introductions to this topic are, of course, possible and would work equally well. As long as you include what needs to be included and leave out what needs to be left out (see the list of "don'ts" a few paragraphs back), then the form your introduction takes is a personal matter.

The Body of the Essay

When you begin to write the main body of your essay (Parts II–V in the basic outline), you need to lay out all of your premises fairly early on. If you need to provide reasons for believing those premises, do that later. First say "here is my argument," and then say "and here are my reasons for thinking that the premises are true and that the premises combine to prove the truth of the conclusion." At the outset, the reader needs to know where you are going and how you are structuring your argument and also have a general overview of the entire argument.

As you can see, the more detailed your outline is, the easier this part of the essay will be to write. In my outline for the essay on ownership of private property, I said, in a fairly specific way, not only what the argument was but also why the premises were true. Writing that part of the essay will just be a matter of putting the pieces together with the appropriate transitions and evidence.

The body of the essay is, of course, the meat of the essay. Chapter 5 has a number of examples of different kinds of arguments, as well as ways arguments can go wrong. If you insure that you don't make any of those mistakes, you'll be in good shape. Using the sample arguments in Chapter 5 as well as other chapters and the argumentative essays that you have undoubtedly read as assignments for your course, you should have a pretty good idea of how to put together this part of the essay.

The Conclusion

There are several ways to conclude your essay. If your essay is very short (2–3 pages), you may simply end it with the final point that leads up to your conclusion. However, even short essays can benefit from a very brief summary of what you have tried to prove. Certainly if your essay is very long or complex, you should provide a summary or review of the main points of your argument. This brings closure for the reader and helps him to better follow your reasoning as well as reminding him of where you started and how you got to the conclusion.

On the other hand, your conclusion can and sometimes should go beyond just summarizing your argument. If you close with "First I said this, and then I showed how it led to that, and then I proved that between them they required that the other was true . . . ," you are going to put your reader to sleep. While you need to close with your main point, you can also go beyond it in various ways.

One way to end an essay is to show what the further implications of your thesis are. In the outline for the essay on ownership of private property, I indicated that in my conclusion I was going to point out that if my thesis is true, then we are going to have to make some radical changes to how our society operates. If we can't own private property, then the way people are paid for their work, and the way goods are distributed will have to change. Another way to end the essay is to mention that what I have been arguing leads to other problems, but that this is a subject for another essay.

Your conclusion should certainly reflect what has been going on in the rest of the essay. You should not introduce any new information or any important new ideas at this point. If you do, you don't leave yourself room to discuss these new points, which can leave your reader hanging. But certainly you should keep your conclusion short and use your final paragraph(s) to provide a satisfying finish and a sense of completeness or closure for your reader.

CONCLUDING REMARKS

While arguing for your own theory or position is more difficult than criticizing someone else's theory, it can also be more rewarding. Of course, by creating your own argument, you open yourself up to criticism by others. Making Parts IV and V thorough and comprehensive should preempt some of that criticism. If you follow the suggestions in this chapter, your synthesis essay should be *relatively* easy to write and you should avoid any *big* mistakes.

SAMPLE ESSAY

The following is an actual essay that a student wrote for a course in Philosophy of Law. This essay was written for an in-class essay examination in answer to the following question:

> Critically discuss whether, in the writings of Ronald Dworkin and Roberto Unger, the concept of autonomy can be used to gain insight into the concept of moral rights (i.e. moral rights that ought to be protected by a legal system.)

Since the essay is not a formal paper and was written under time constraint, the essay is not as polished as it might be. In particular, it doesn't really conform to the outline suggested in this chapter. Writing an essay in the classroom usually involves leaving out (or greatly abbreviating) introduction, conclusion, and sometimes even responses to criticism. This essay is essentially a compare/contrast essay on two writers, including the author's own position. It is hardly perfect. However, the author does a good job of laying out both positions and showing how they differ.

Here's the essay:

Autonomy and Moral Rights

According to Dworkin, the central problem in law is the conflict between the right to liberty and the right to equality. A person has a right to liberty in a weak sense—that is, if it is in his interests to have it (i.e. he wants it, or he would be better off with it.) In this weak sense, Dworkin says, people have a right to liberty as well as, for example, a right to vanilla ice cream. The right to equality is a much stronger right. A person has a right to equality not merely because he wants it, but because he is *entitled* to it. It is wrong for the government to deny something a person has right to in the strong sense, *even if* it would be in the general interest to do so. This anti-utilitarian sense of right, according to Dworkin, is the sense utilized in the U.S. Constitution.

The right to equality, Dworkin says, requires that the government treat people with *concern* (as human beings capable of suffering), and with *respect* (as human beings capable of deciding on and choosing how to live their lives—i.e. *autonomous*.) That is, people should be treated not only with concern and respect, but also with *equal* concern and respect. People, he says, must be treated as autonomous creatures, and that is accomplished in two ways. First, people have the right to **equal treatment** (e.g. one vote per person) and second, people have a right to **treatment as equals**. Treatment as equals does not imply a right to equal distribution of goods and opportunities, but a right to equal concern and respect in the political decision about how the goods and opportunities are to be distributed. The right to treatment as equals, Dworkin says, is more fundamental than the right to equal treatment. The right to equal treatment only holds when it follows from the right to treatment as equals.

Dworkin says that the right to liberty should not be understood in the same strong sense as the right to equality. People do not have a right to liberty in the strong sense. Although, for example, a law that forbids me to drive north on Lexington Avenue diminishes my liberty, it does not violate any rights. I have no *right* to drive north on Lexington Avenue. Many laws that infringe on my liberty can be justified on Utilitarian grounds (it would be best for all if Lexington Avenue is one way going south.) But, Dworkin says, although I do not have a general right to liberty in the strong sense, I do have a right to some individual liberties and *not* on Utilitarian grounds. In fact, it might not be for the greater good for people to have the right to free speech, for example. One reason, according to Dworkin, why we have these rights to specific liberties is because they follow from the very strong right we have to be treated as equals—that is, as autonomous individuals. Part of the implication of the right to treatment as equals is that, in respect for the individual's right to choose how to live her life, etc., political decisions must be, as far as possible, independent of any particular conception of the good life. Each person has her own conception of the good life, and if the government prefers any one conception to any other, then it is not treating people as equals.

So, for Dworkin, the rights that people have, that should be protected by the legal system, are any and all that follow from treating people as autonomous creatures—that is, treating people as equals. Any specific right must follow from the strong general right to treatment as equals. No individual liberty can ever *override* the right to treatment as equals; each is allowable, and should be protected, only when it follows from the right to treatment as equals.

For Unger, a system of rights is meant to describe the relative positions of individuals within institutional arrangements; it is meant to encourage some dealings between people and discourage others. There are, he says, essentially four categories of rights:

1. immunity rights—the nearly absolute claim of the individual to security against the government, organizations or institutions, and other people. These include political and civil rights, welfare, right to withdrawal from the society, etc.

2. destabilization rights—claims to the disruption of institutions and social practices that contribute to discrimination, etc.

3. market rights—claims to divisible portions of social property (but, he says, there are no absolute property rights)

4. solidarity rights—legal entitlements to expectations raised by communal life (good faith, loyalty, expectations fostered, etc.)

So, where does autonomy come in? I don't know that Unger ever actually uses the word, but if you follow a conception of autonomy like Dworkin's, it is clear that the four categories of rights are meant to protect the autonomy of the individual. When Unger talks about the equal protection principle, he seems to have in mind something like Dworkin's "treatment as equals." The equal protection principle has two tasks. First, it must be *generality-requiring*—that is, it must impede any action against individuals (i.e. respect their autonomy). Second, it must be *generality-correcting* (destabilization rights)—it must prevent the establishment or reinforcement of any collective disadvantages and it must cure or alleviate exceptional and irremediable cases of collective disadvantage.

According to Unger, a person's life chances and experiences should be freed from the tyranny of abstract social categories. She should not be the puppet of her place in the contrast of classes, sexes, or nations. That is, I think, she must be respected as an equal, autonomous person. Unger is much more specific about how the legal system should work, while Dworkin is more theoretical. Yet they seem to be saying much the same thing. A person has a right (that ought to be protected by a legal system) when that right follows from her autonomy. Dworkin, I think, fares better in this endeavor since he attempts to show how specific rights follow from autonomy. Unger (since he's more a legal type than a philosopher, this may not be surprising) focuses more on what the rights are, rather than where they come from.

In any case, I think Dworkin is right about where our rights come from. It seems clear that some rights can't (and shouldn't) be justified on Utilitarian grounds. If we are to have a specific right, it should follow from the treatment of the individual as an autonomous individual. I agree with Dworkin that the autonomous choice of the individual is important in and of itself, and as a result, the government can't impose its values or judgements on society.

8

USING RESEARCH IN A
POLITICAL SCIENCE PAPER

A **research paper** is any paper for which you are expected to find and read material from sources other than your textbook. Most essays are not, and should not be, research papers. You can't go to the library to discover whether property should be privately owned, whether democracy is the best form of government, or whether capital punishment is justified. You *can* go to the library to find out what *other* people have thought about these issues, but unless your instructor explicitly assigns a research paper, this is not what she intends for you to do. These "truths" are not things we look up in books; they are truths we acquire by a lot of hard thinking. If you merely report what someone else thinks, then you are not doing that thinking for yourself. In addition, you may be guilty of plagiarism, a serious offense that will be discussed later in this chapter.

A research paper in political science is generally an essay in which you take a position on some topic and then review what others have said about it. Some of them may agree with you, others will disagree. The point is, however, that a research paper is typically supposed to be original. Rarely will a professor ask you *merely* to report what others have said about your topic. Usually you are expected to present an argument for your position, and then use your research to provide counter-arguments to your position, or to present arguments in support of your position.

SOURCES

There are two different kinds of sources that you may use in your research paper: primary and secondary. A **primary source** is a book or article that is an author's own original work about your topic. **Secondary sources** are books or articles that have been written by other people *about* the author or book or essay that is the primary source. In other words, if you are writing about Rousseau's *Social Contract*, then that book is your primary source. Your secondary sources will be books and essays in which other people write about Rousseau's *Social Contract*. If you look up Rousseau in an encyclopedia, you will find an article written about him. If you look up Aristotle's six forms of political government in an encyclopedia of politics, you will find an article explaining what the six forms of government are and what Aristotle says about them. These are secondary sources. If your textbook is an anthology of original sources (that is, excerpts of books or essays by Locke or Aristotle or Mill), then those excerpts are primary sources. If, on the other hand, your textbook is the kind of book which *tells* you what Locke or Aristotle or Mill said, then that is a secondary source.

While you will use both kinds of sources for your research paper, notice what the word "primary" means. Your *primary* source is the main or principal source for your essay. The *secondary* sources are just that—secondary. Students are often tempted to do their research in the secondary literature before they have done their own thinking about the topic. Don't do this! Even in a research paper, you should be writing an original essay and using research merely to provide support for your position. If you cram your brain with what other people have to say about your topic, there is going to be little room for you to do your own thinking. Before you begin your research, try writing a summary of what you plan to say in your essay. Once you have a pretty firm grasp on what you want to say, then you are ready to begin looking for other sources. After you begin your research, it is possible that you will change your mind about some things, but try to figure it out for yourself first.

In looking for sources, a good place to start is Appendix B, which lists a number of sources for political science research essays. Use the indexes in these books. Look up the author of the work you are writing about, as well as various keywords.

One thing you will find, even in the books listed in Appendix B, is that you will not always be able to understand everything you read. Articles in political science journals can be rather advanced for introductory students. If you can't understand them, leave them and go look for something you can better comprehend.

Another thing to realize about writing research essays in political science is that most regular encyclopedias are relatively useless. They are often too general and sometimes too superficial to be adequate as a source. In addition, many of the sources you may have used for other classes, like *The Reader's Guide to Periodical Literature*, will be less helpful for your political science essay. Political scientists don't usually publish in *Time* magazine or *Redbook*, and the journals they do publish in are not indexed in the *Reader's Guide*. Even if you find something in one of the magazines indexed in the *Reader's Guide* that seems to be on your topic, chances are it is not going to be an acceptable source for your essay. *The Social Sciences Index* (see Appendix B) indexes many journals of political science, and it can be helpful. However, there is a good chance that your university library does not carry many of the journals indexed. Also, most journals are intended for other professional scholars and not for undergraduates. Check to see which journals your library carries. Then, as you look at the index, you can make note of only those articles that are actually available to you.

Another place to look for sources is the library's "card catalog"—which generally is not on cards anymore. Most libraries are now cataloged on the computer, which makes searches much easier. Each book is usually listed three times in the catalog—once under the author's or authors' names, once under the title, and one or more times by subject. Search by name, topic, title, and keywords. Any computer keyword search can, of course, be tricky. You may get so many books that you don't have the time to look at them all. You can always narrow your search by adding keywords. For example, instead of searching for "property," you might search for "Locke and property," or even "Locke, property and ownership."

You need to be especially careful about the reliability of your sources. With the advent of the Internet, many students rely on the computer for all of their research. Be very careful when you read things on the Internet to be sure that the author of the information knows what he is talking about. I still remember the day one of my students called me about an essay he was writing on abortion. He started quoting "facts" about the development of the fetus, most of which were inaccurate. I asked him where he got the information, and he said, "Oh, it was on an anti-abortion web page." I gently suggested that a better source about the growth and development of a fetus might be a science textbook. It simply never occurred to him that anything he read could be wrong. While this is a very large problem with web pages, it is also a problem with some books and essays.

The moral of the story is to double-check your sources, particularly if they are making factual claims, and that applies to books, articles, and web pages. Even if the author is a famous author, a professor at Harvard, or your own instructor, don't assume that she has the last word. Just because she thinks, for example, that Locke's argument for private property doesn't work, that doesn't necessarily mean that she is right. Many of the "truths" of political science, as I have already said, must be discovered by you. Simply because someone famous says it is true doesn't mean it is so.

QUOTATION AND PARAPHRASE

In the course of writing any essay, you will probably need to either directly quote what an author has said or paraphrase his ideas. Inexperienced writers often use quotations and paraphrases excessively. If you can state an author's point more briefly than he did, then put his main points into your own words. Quotations should be used sparingly and only for a few reasons. First, if the author has said something so eloquently that paraphrasing it would lose something from the original, then quotation is necessary. Second, if the author says something that you disagree with and want to argue against, you may need to directly quote her in order to show that you have presented her argument fairly. Third, it may be necessary to quote an author to show that he actually said what you claim he said, or to point out his use of various key words and phrases.

However, quotations can't stand on their own in an essay. If you quote a passage, you must comment on and interpret the idea. Explain what it means, why it is significant, how it fits in with the rest of your argument, and why your reader should take it seriously. The point of asking you to write an essay is to show your instructor that you understand some essay, argument, or theory. When you quote an author, all you show is that you are able to read and copy a passage. Quoting a passage does not show that you understand it.

Be very careful that your quotations aren't too long. An overlong quotation can overwhelm the point you are trying to make. Also, you want to avoid what I call a "cut-and-paste" essay, or what one teacher calls a "model plane" essay.[1] The model plane essay occurs when the writer takes a little from this source, a quote from that source, and some ideas from another source, and glues them all together with a few sentences of her own. While it can sometimes make for an elegant and clever "model plane," it's still a model plane—just like the one anyone else could put together. There is not enough in it that is original for your instructor to regard it as your own work. A paper that is merely a patchwork of other people's words will not be thought of very highly (or

---

[1] Richard Marius, *A Writer's Companion*, 3rd ed. (New York: McGraw-Hill, 1995), p. 171.

graded very highly) by your instructor. Here's an example of what *not* to do:

> Broad claims that judgments which profess to be about the future don't refer to any fact at the time they are made (Healey, 111), even though "it is possible for anyone who understands their meaning to see what kind of fact will make them true or false as the case may be" (Gale, 236). They have a present truth-or-falsity, but they are not presently true or false, "and so they *cannot* be known; there is not really anything to be known" (Dummett, 338). These statements will become true or false, Broad says, when there is a fact for them to refer to (Broad, 112).

Not only does this paragraph make little sense, since it is a series of quotes and paraphrases strung together, there is no indication that the *writer* has any idea what it means either.

Think very carefully about your purpose for quoting a passage. Don't quote merely to keep from having to do your own thinking. Don't quote merely to show your instructor that you've read the book (she'll take that for granted). Above all, don't quote merely to take up space. And keep your quotations short. Any quotation that consists of two or more sentences or runs to four or more lines should be indented and single spaced, with no quotation marks. Here, for example, is a lengthy quote from John Stuart Mill's *Utilitarianism*:

> The creed which accepts as the foundation of morals, Utility, or the Greatest Happiness Principle, holds that actions are right in proportion as they tend to promote happiness, wrong as they tend to produce the reverse of happiness. By happiness is intended pleasure, and the absence of pain; by unhappiness, pain, and the privation of pleasure. To give a clear view of the moral standard set up by the theory, much more requires to be said; in particular, what things it includes in the ideas of pain and pleasure; and to what extent this is left an open question.[2]

It is usually better not to use such block quotations if you can help it. Better that you paraphrase the passage, and only use some shorter quotations if necessary.

This quotation from the passage above utilizes ellipsis marks to make the passage more concise:

> The Greatest Happiness Principle . . . holds that actions are right in proportion as they tend to promote happiness, wrong as they tend to

---

[2] John Stuart Mill, *Utilitarianism*, Chapter II, "What Utilitarianism Is" (London: Parker, Son and Bourn, 1863).

produce the reverse of happiness. By happiness is intended pleasure, and the absence of pain; by unhappiness, pain, and the privation of pleasure.

Ellipsis marks are the three little dots (. . .) used to show that something has been left out in the middle. Be careful, when you do this, not to alter the author's meaning. By leaving words out in this passage, I have not changed the meaning. However, consider the following passage, also from Mill's *Utilitarianism*:

> Now, such a theory of life excites in many minds, and among them in some of the most estimable in feeling and purpose, inveterate dislike. To suppose that life has (as they express it) no higher end than pleasure- no better and nobler object of desire and pursuit- they designate as utterly mean and grovelling; as a doctrine worthy only of swine, to whom the followers of Epicurus were, at a very early period, contemptuously likened; and modern holders of the doctrine are occasionally made the subject of equally polite comparisons by its German, French, and English assailants.[3]

Now consider the following "condensation" of that passage:

> Such a theory of life . . . [is] utterly mean and grovelling . . . a doctrine worthy only of swine.

(Notice my use of brackets to insert the word "is" in order to make the sentence grammatical.) In the original passage, Mill does not claim that the Greatest Happiness Principle is bad. Yet that is what the "condensed" version of the passage says. If you make any claims or assertions about Mill's argument based on this inaccurate quotation, your conclusions are likely to be wrong because you have distorted Mill's claims. So you can see why it is important that, when you leave words, phrases, or whole sentences out, the resulting quotation does not misrepresent the original meaning of the passage.

Never begin a sentence with a quotation mark. Quotations require lead-ins, which are your own words or phrases that tie the quotation to the rest of the text both logically and stylistically. To use the previous passage as an example, one way to use a lead-in is like this:

> However, Mill admits that "such a theory of life . . . ."

Another example of a lead-in involves positioning a quote in the middle of a sentence, with your own words before and after it. For example:

---

[3] Mill, *Utilitarianism*, Chapter II.

> However, Mill admits that "such a theory of life excites in many minds . . . inveterate dislike," but in this, he says they are wrong.

Quotations should flow with the rest of your text and not stick out like a sore thumb. Often that means that you need to use a lead-in and/or a follow-through, by surrounding the quotation with your own words as in the example above.

PLAGIARISM

When you use someone else's words or ideas and do not properly cite them, you are committing **plagiarism**. Plagiarism is stealing, plain and simple. You have stolen the words or ideas of someone who invested his time and energy in developing them. Plagiarism is also a kind of deception: You have deceived your instructor by implying that these thoughts and ideas are your own. And finally, when you plagiarize, you wrong yourself: You have not done the work assigned and have not learned what the assignment was supposed to teach you.

Consider the two previous passages from Mill's *Utilitarianism*. Suppose that within the text of my essay I say the following:

> Such a theory of life (i.e. the principle of utility) excites many minds to see it as utterly mean and groveling and a doctrine only worthy of swine.

Unless this is clearly an essay about Mill, and unless I explicitly give credit to Mill (perhaps by beginning the passage with a statement like "Here is Mill's statement of objections"), then I have committed plagiarism. By not acknowledging that this is Mill's idea (even though I haven't used any of his exact words), I have suggested that this is my own original idea. That constitutes plagiarism.

The most common examples of plagiarism that I have come across, however, concern representing a secondary source's criticisms of an author or theory as your own. Suppose you are writing an essay about Mill's argument in *Utilitarianism* concerning the principle of utility. Further suppose that you want to argue that Mill is wrong and that his argument is fundamentally flawed. At this point, many students head for a secondary source to see what someone else thought was wrong with Mill's argument. Then they write their essay using someone else's argument, without giving that person credit for the idea. This is plagiarism. You are falsely claiming that something is your own idea, when in reality you have stolen it from someone else. Even if you do not directly quote a source, you must give credit where credit is due. When you paraphrase a passage, use a citation to give credit to the author. When you borrow an idea or argument, cite the source. Otherwise, you are committing plagiarism.

Plagiarism is a serious academic offense that can be punished by failure on the essay, failure in the class, or, in the extreme, suspension or expulsion from school. Don't do it! Be sure you understand how to avoid it.

CITATIONS

Any time you use either words or ideas from something you have read, you must acknowledge the source by using some kind of **citation**. At the very least, you must mention the author's name—So-and-so claims such-and-such. If you have used the author's exact words, you must also use quotation marks. Ask your instructor which kind of citation he prefers. If he does not express a preference, follow the examples in this section.

The most common kind of citation is the **footnote**. A superscript number at the end of the quote refers the reader to the bottom of the page where the number is repeated with a citation. Here is an example.[4] Another alternative is to use endnotes. **Endnotes** look exactly like footnotes, but instead of each being at the bottom of the page, they are listed together at the end of the essay, chapter, or book.

To cite a book, whether in a footnote or endnote, you should include the author's name, the name of the essay or book, where it was published, the name of the publisher, when it was published, and the number of the page from which you quoted. Some examples follow.

- *A single author book:*

  [1]Hugo Adam Bedau, *Making Mortal Choices: Three Exercises in Moral Casuistry* (New York: Oxford University Press, 1997), p. 56.

  According to this footnote, the material you quoted or paraphrased is found on page 56 of Hugo Bedau's book, *Making Mortal Choices*.

- *A book with several authors:*

  [2]William R. Maples, Ph.D., and Michael Browning, *Dead Men Do Tell Tales: The Strange and Fascinating Cases of a Forensic Anthropologist* (New York: Doubleday, 1994), p. 191.

---

[4] Notice how the footnote is at the bottom of the page to make it easy to find.

- *A book with a translator:*
     ³René Descartes, *Meditations on First Philosophy*, trans. Donald A. Cress (Indianapolis: Hackett Publishing Company, Inc., 1979), p. 13.

- *A book with an editor:*
     ⁴William James, *Pragmatism*, ed. Bruce Kuklick (Indianapolis: Hackett Publishing Company, Inc., 1981), p. 36.

- *A single essay from a collection:*
     ⁵Monte Cook, "Tips for Time Travel" *in Philosophers Look at Science Fiction*, ed. Nicholas D. Smith (Chicago: Nelson-Hall, 1982), pp. 54–55.

- *A journal article:*
     ⁶Jonathan Harrison, "Dr Who and the Philosophers or Time-Travel for Beginners," *Proceedings of The Aristotelian Society*, supplementary volume XLV (1971), p. 24.

- *A signed article in an encyclopedia:*
     ⁷A.D. Woozley, "Universals," *Encyclopedia of Philosophy*, Paul Edwards, ed. (New York: MacMillan Publishing Co., Inc. & The Free Press, 1967).

- *An Internet citation:*
     ⁸Tom Buerkle, "Cloning of Humans? Unethical, EU Panel Decides." <http://www.iht.com/IHT/TB/97/tb053097.html>. May 30, 1997.

Note that for an Internet citation, the entire web address (inside the < > brackets) should be on one line. If it won't fit on one line, it should, at least, begin on a separate line.

When you have already cited a source once with a complete footnote reference, later citations need only the author's name and page number. Thus,

     ⁹James, p. 59

refers to page 59 of the James book (footnote 4). If you need to cite something not listed here, consult either Kate Turabian's *excellent Manual For Writers*⁵ or *The Chicago Manual of Style*.⁶

An alternative to using footnotes or endnotes is to use **a parenthetical reference**. Instead of using a superscript footnote number after the

---

⁵ Kate L. Turabian, *A Manual for Writers of Term Papers, Theses, and Dissertations*, 5th ed., revised and expanded by Bonnie Birtwistle Honigsblum (Chicago: The University of Chicago Press, 1987).
⁶ *The Chicago Manual of Style: for authors, editors and copywriters*, 13th ed. (Chicago: The University of Chicago Press, 1983).

quote, parentheses are used with a shortened form of the citation. If your instructor does not require footnotes or endnotes, use the parenthetical reference. It is shorter, easier to type (unless your computer word processing program does footnotes for you), and, most importantly as far as I'm concerned, it is much easier on your reader. Here is an example of a parenthetical reference using a quote from page 13 of Mill's *Utilitarianism*: "When thus attacked, the Epicureans have always answered, that it is not they, but their accusers, who represent human nature in a degrading light; since the accusation supposes human beings to be capable of no pleasures except those of which swine are capable." (Mill 13). Notice that the parenthetical reference is placed after the quotation marks and before the period. If you use the parenthetical reference on a block quotation (which doesn't have quotation marks, remember), the reference should go after the period. If you have mentioned the author's name in your lead-in to the quotation, then the reference would just be a page number: (13). If you have two books or essays by the same author, then you should use the author's name, the year it was published, and the page number, thus: (Mill 1863, 13). Along with your parenthetical reference, then, you will need a reference list. The form for your **reference list** is similar to the form of a footnote:

> John Stuart Mill. 1863. *Utilitarianism.* London: Parker, Son and Bourn.

The information is the same; it is just in slightly different order. The same, of course, is true for other kinds of references. So some of the earlier references would look thus:

> Cook, Monte. 1982. *Tips for Time Travel. In Philosophers Look at Science Fiction*, ed. Nicholas D. Smith, pp. 47–55. Chicago: Nelson-Hall.

> Woozley, A. D. 1967. Universals. *Encyclopedia of Philosophy*, ed. Paul Edwards. New York: MacMillan Publishing Co., Inc. & The Free Press.

Sources should be listed alphabetically by the author's last name.

BIBLIOGRAPHY

If you have quoted or cited any sources, you probably need a bibliography. A **bibliography** is a list of the books, articles, and journals that you have read in preparing your essay. Therefore, you may need a bibliography, even if you don't have any direct quotes. I recommend to students that any primary or secondary source they read to develop their own ideas and their essay should be listed in the bibliography. Even if you didn't consciously borrow any ideas, it is probably safer to go ahead and list the essay or book. If you have used the full version of footnotes or endnotes as shown above, then you may not need a bibliography. If you used parenthetical references, you will have a reference list instead of a bibliography. (See above for the form of the reference list.) The form of a bibliography is slightly different from a reference list:

> Cook, Monte. "Tips for Time Travel." In Philosophers Look at Science Fiction, ed. Nicholas D. Smith, pp. 47–55. Chicago: Nelson-Hall, 1982.

> Woozley, A. D. "Universals," Encyclopedia of Philosophy, ed. Paul Edwards. New York: MacMillan Publishing Co., Inc. & The Free Press, 1967.

In a bibliography, as with the reference list, sources should be ordered alphabetically by the author's last name. There's not much difference between the two, and many instructors don't care either way. The key is to make sure that you give enough information about the source, so that your readers can look up the original passage if they want to. Therefore, in some form or other, you must provide author, title, editor or translator if relevant, publisher, copyright date, and page numbers. Remember, when in doubt about what form of citation or bibliography to use, check with your instructor.

CONCLUDING REMARKS

Be sure that you are careful about citing sources and including bibliographic information. Others may want to check some of your sources or even read them for themselves. By using accurate citations and references, you not only preempt any accusation of plagiarism, but you also give credit for ideas, thoughts, and theories where credit is due—that is, to their authors.

9

PUTTING PENCIL TO PAPER (OR FINGERS TO KEYBOARD)

GETTING STARTED

The most valuable piece of advice about writing essays that you will ever receive is this: Just do it. As soon as an essay is assigned, start thinking about it and planning what you want to say. Whether the paper is due next week or next month or at the end of the semester, don't wait until the night or the week before it is due to start thinking about it. Begin your research (if necessary) and your planning and organizing right away. The more you think about the essay, the easier it will be to write when the time comes. However, don't spend so much time planning and researching that you put off writing until the last minute. The sooner you begin the writing, the more time you will have for editing and revising.

Make sure you completely understand the assignment. Read any instructions provided by the instructor. Ask questions. You can't write an "A" paper (or even a "B" or "C" paper) if you don't write the kind of paper your instructor has assigned. Of course, following the directions doesn't guarantee a good paper, but not following them does guarantee a poor one.

If your instructor allows you to choose your own topic, choose carefully! You need to strike a balance between a topic you find completely uninteresting and one that you feel so passionately about that you can't be objective about it. In either case, you will find it difficult to write clearly and constructively. If your instructor does not give you any guidance on possible topics, it is probably best if you choose a topic that directly relates to the material covered in class or your text. Even if your instructor does not require you to do so, you should get her approval for your topic. You don't want to spend your time writing on a topic your instructor considers unacceptable.

It is sometimes a good idea to word your topic as a question. Your essay, then, attempts to answer that question. For example, instead of choosing "Mill's *On Liberty*" as a topic (which you couldn't, in any case, cover adequately in a short essay), choose one small part of it and formulate it as a question:

> Why does Mill argue that liberty of thought and expression should be almost absolute?

In addition, it may be helpful to express your topic in a more formal way. I usually have students hand in a paper topic based on the following:

My paper topic is _____.

I intend to argue (or show) that _____,

because _____.

The advantage of this format is that once you fill in the blanks, you know what your thesis or conclusion is, so you know what you need to prove in the rest of your essay. This form can be adapted to a number of the essays illustrated in this book. For example:

Application essay: My paper topic is <u>Socrates's argument about civil disobedience</u>. I intend to show that <u>when applied to draft dodging, Socrates would say that one should not dodge the draft</u>, because <u>doing so would be reneging on your agreement to obey the laws in return for enjoying the benefits of society</u>.

Analysis essay: My paper topic is <u>John Stuart Mill's argument regarding the connection between justice and utility</u>. I intend to show that <u>his argument shows that justice is an important part of utility</u>, because <u>justice is just a name we give to certain kinds of things that make us very happy</u>.

Evaluation essay: My paper topic is <u>Robert Nozick's argument that the "night-watchman" state is the only one that does not violate individual rights</u>. I intend to argue that <u>Nozick is right</u>, because <u>although</u>

<dl>
<dd>

no form of government is entirely satisfactory, the alternatives to the night-watchman state have disadvantages that outweigh their advantages.
</dd>
</dl>

Synthesis essay:
My paper topic is which form of government—direct democracy or representative democracy—is better. I intend to argue that representative democracy is better, because larger states can accomplish more, and direct democracy is impossible in any but the very smallest states.

The important thing to remember is that you can't write well about a topic that you don't understand, aren't interested in, or is either too broad or too narrow. It bears repeating—if you choose your own topic, be sure you check with your instructor to make sure you are on the right track.

Before you begin writing, review your class notes and any notes you took when reading the assignment. Reread the essay or argument that you are writing about. Make some notes to yourself about how you plan to proceed. If some points are not clear, consult a specialized dictionary or an encyclopedia of political science (see Appendix B). Preparing an outline (see Chapters 6 and 7 for hints) is very helpful.

Finally, begin writing. Once you start, stay with it for at least an hour. Begin, keep going, and don't get discouraged. Just get your ideas on paper. However, you don't have to write the whole essay at one sitting. If it helps, begin by writing a short summary of what you intend to say—perhaps a quarter or a third the length that the essay is supposed to be. Once you get on paper the major points you want to make, you can go back and fill in the details. Don't try to edit or revise as you go along. If you can't think of the right word, just leave a blank space and keep going. If you don't like the way you've phrased something, circle it and go on. If you think a word is misspelled, circle it so that you can look it up later. Don't worry about commas, spelling, and so on, at this stage. The important thing is that you get started and continue until you have a rough draft written.

Depending on what kind of essay you are writing, consult the appropriate chapter of this book for guidelines on content. Writing a first draft isn't easy. Be sure you give yourself plenty of time. Don't worry if your first draft is wordy or rambles or doesn't seem to make the points you want to make. First drafts are expected to have problems—that's why they are first drafts and are followed by *second* and *third* and sometimes *fourth* and *fifth* drafts. In a first draft you are just trying to get your ideas written down. This is not the time to criticize your thoughts and arguments. Save your criticism for later revisions.

You should write your essay so that a reasonably intelligent person with no background in political science can make sense of it. Don't assume too much on the part of the reader. Yes, your instructor presumably knows all about the subject, almost certainly more than you do, but the point of writing an essay is for the instructor to discover what you know about the subject. If you assume too much knowledge on the part of your reader, your instructor can't be sure that you know what has been left out. Your job is to prove to her that you understand what she already knows. Let a roommate, spouse, sibling, or friend read your essay. If he can't understand what you are trying to say, then you need to go back and revise so that he can.

Consider writing your introduction and conclusion last. A good introduction presents your main points and indicates where your essay is going, while a good conclusion wraps it all up and shows where you have been. Realistically, you may not know exactly where your essay is going until you finish writing it. Even if you don't wait until the end to write the introduction and conclusion, you should be sure you do some serious rewriting to bring them in line with what you have actually said in the essay (as opposed to what you *meant* to say or *thought* you said).

REWRITING

Above all, don't plan to turn in your first draft. Just as you had to reread the essay or argument you are writing about, so you will have to rewrite the essay you are writing. Rewrite, rewrite, and rewrite some more. Realize, however, that rewriting doesn't mean just correcting misplaced commas or misspelled words. Rewriting means revising—that is, possibly making radical changes in your first draft. You may need to rearrange or even delete whole paragraphs. You may find that you need to add sentences or paragraphs to make your essay more intelligible. Be ruthless about removing sentences that don't fit or paragraphs that are incoherent. Don't pad your essay with irrelevancies. Don't ramble. If you did not begin with an outline, or if you have departed from your original outline, then when you finish your first draft, try outlining it. An outline will help show you where your thought processes are going wrong. Straighten out problems in organization and clarity before you begin worrying about commas and sentence fragments.

On the other hand, don't assume that grammar doesn't matter. Instructors expect correct punctuation, complete sentences, and accurate spelling. Of course, an essay that is grammatically correct and neatly typed is not necessarily a good essay, but don't think that having good ideas and arguments will make up for bad spelling, bad grammar, and messiness. When you do not observe the conventions of good grammar, your instructor is likely to think that you are careless, illiterate, or even dim-witted. She may also assume that you don't care enough about the class, your grade, or her to do your best work. Reading essays that are grammatically incorrect, vague, rambling, or even obscure to the point of unintelligibility is distracting, irritating, and confusing—regardless of how "profound" you think your ideas are. The fundamental goal of writing is communication with the reader and grammatical sloppiness will frustrate that goal.

After you finish a draft, put the paper aside for a couple of days, if you can. If you don't have that much time, at least leave it for a few hours. When you come back fresh to your essay, you may find that things that seemed perfectly clear originally now seem incoherent, that the connections between paragraphs are unclear or nonexistent, or even that parts of the essay are much better than you thought. Leaving the essay alone for a few days gives you a fresh perspective that can be very helpful when you begin revising.

At this point, it may be helpful to have someone else read and comment on your essay. Because you know what you are trying to say, it is sometimes difficult to get the distance necessary to be objective about your own work. Be sure that whoever reads it for you is aware of what constitutes good writing and knows the rules of grammar. Make sure the person you've asked to read your essay is willing to criticize. It won't help much if he says, "Wow, I really liked your essay." If your best friend is reluctant to criticize your writing, choose someone else. Many colleges offer free writing advice through writing centers. You need constructive criticism. Ask your reader what she thinks you are trying to say. Ask her to tell you why she agrees or disagrees with you. The point is to get some comments that will help you to improve your essay. However, don't automatically assume your reader is right. Think about her criticism carefully, but, in the end, rely on your own judgment.

PROBLEMS TO AVOID

When you revise your essay, watch out for the following common problems.

Don't Assume That Just Because Someone Famous Said It, It Must Be So

In political science, we are inclined to think that no one is enough of an authority to have the last word on a subject. Quoting an authority is not a substitute for an argument. An authority's opinion is simply another opinion. While Locke's opinion on a subject, for example, may carry some weight, it generally isn't enough. You must provide other evidence for thinking he is right.

Use an Objective Tone

Most college papers should be written with an objective tone that avoids preachiness, inflammatory or emotional language, cliches or colloquialisms, and silliness. Many instructors will tell you never to use *you* or *I* in an essay. I instruct students not to use either one excessively, but tell them that occasionally either or both can be appropriate. Since many essays involve your opinion or evaluation of a subject, it is difficult to avoid saying *I*. However, don't get in the way of your subject. Too many *Is* indicate that the subject of your essay is you rather than your political science topic. If you do use *you* be sure you only use it in reference to the reader. Most uses of *you* can be revised by replacing the word you with *the reader* or *one* or even *they*. In any case, be sure to check with your instructor for his preferences regarding *you* and *I*. Even if he allows them, you should use them sparingly.

Use the Correct Words

Be sure that you don't equivocate on the meaning of words in your essay. If, for example, you use the words *democracy* or *communism*, be sure that you make it clear to the reader exactly what you mean by them. Chances are that the authors you quote will use these words in different ways as well. Clarify each different meaning. Unless everyone is using *democracy* in the same way, confusion will result. Benito Mussolini, for example, once claimed that his fascism was "the purest form of democracy";[1] Karl Marx said much the same thing about his socialism.[2] Obviously they are using different definitions of democracy. Unless you explain these different meanings, your essay will be incomprehensible to the reader.

Be Charitable

Remember the principle of charity discussed in Chapter 2. Give the author whose theory you are writing about the benefit of the doubt. If one interpretation of his theory seems ridiculous, and another is at least

---

[1] Benito Mussolini, "The Doctrine of Fascism," in *Classic Philosophical Questions*, 8th ed., James Gould, ed. (Englewood Cliffs, NJ: Prentice Hall, 1995), p. 557.

[2] Karl Marx and Friedrich Engels, "Manifesto of the Communist Party," *in Revolution from 1789 to 1906*, R. W. Postgate, ed. (New York: Harper Torchbooks, 1962), p. 154.

fairly reasonable, then, all other things being equal, you should assume that the latter interpretation is correct. Remember that however much you disagree with an author, he would not have written what he did if he did not think he was being reasonable. And he would probably not have been published if others did not believe he had something valuable to say. Writers often make unfair and offensive remarks or insults about a theory or idea when they don't understand it very well or they are unsure about their own position and thus feel threatened. Showing respect for an author and his work, whether you agree with it or not, is the least you can do.

Distinguish the Arguer from the Argument

Don't fall into the trap of arguing that because Jean-Paul Sartre, for example, is an atheist, then his political theory must be wrong. Don't attack the *arguer* instead of the *argument*. Sartre's atheism has nothing to do with how good his argument is. We are primarily interested in *arguments*. If you disagree with an author's argument, you have to work out carefully the reasons why you disagree. You can't get out of it by merely saying, "He's a lousy sort of character, so I can ignore him." This is an unfair (and unethical) way to object to an argument.

Don't Use Sexist Language

Use gender-neutral language to avoid offending your reader. Instead of *mankind,* say *humanity.* Instead of *man,* say *person.* Don't use masculine pronouns when you are referring to groups that include both males and females. Instead of using *he* and *him* (unless, of course, you are talking about a specific person who is male), consider revising the sentence to use *they* and *them.* If you can't use a plural pronoun, then you should probably alternate *she* and *he.* (Notice how I have done so in this book.)

Exclude Irrelevant Facts

Students are often tempted to include in their essays historical background or personal facts about an author. Unless these facts are directly relevant to the author's conclusions, omit them. On the other hand, don't exclude relevant facts just because your reader (the instructor) already knows them.

Don't Write Too Little

If your draft is too short, ask yourself: Have I clearly explained the theory or policy that I am writing about? Have I supported my main points? Have I provided arguments for why those points are correct, instead of simply stating them? Have I provided examples to illustrate my main points? If you have done all this and your essay is still too short, then your topic may be too narrow. However, if your instructor has assigned the topic, then you haven't answered some or all of these questions thoroughly enough.

Don't Write Too Much

If your draft is too long, your topic may be too broad, you may have included too much extraneous material, or you may be rambling. Longer is not necessarily better. A draft that is too long may indicate that you have very little to say about the topic and are just filling space with background or too many and too lengthy examples. Your instructor won't be fooled! On the other hand, a draft that is too long may indicate that you need to make your topic narrower. If you try to cover Aristotle's entire political theory in five pages, you are almost certain to fail.

THE FINAL EDIT

When you have finished revising, do your final edit. The best way to edit for grammar is to read your essay aloud. Read slowly and listen to the sound of the sentences. Often your ear will detect errors that your eyes have missed. Be sure you read exactly what is on the page. Because you wrote the essay, you may automatically fill in what you meant to say. Ask a friend to read it to you while you listen, or read it into a tape recorder and then play it back. If you haven't already done so, you might want to get help from your school's writing center, if it has one.

Before you type or print your final draft, *look* at your paper. How long are your paragraphs? A good rule of thumb is that a paragraph should have a minimum of three or four sentences, but it shouldn't take up a whole page. All your paragraphs don't need to be the same length, but neither should they hit the extremes. An average page will probably have two or three paragraphs. Also, look at the length of your sentences. Shorter sentences are easier to read, but if they are too short your essay will sound like "See Spot run. Run, Spot, run." Don't make sentences too long, either. Your reader must be able to follow the sentence to the bitter end. If you have written a sentence that seems to be out of control, chances are you are probably trying to express a thought that is out of control. Divide long and complex sentences into several shorter, clearer, and more concise sentences. When you read your essay aloud, you will probably hear these trouble spots.

If you are at all concerned that a word is misspelled, look it up in a dictionary. If you are using a computer, use the spell-check function. If your word processing program includes a grammar checker as well, use it. However, don't rely too heavily on either. If you use the wrong word (but spell it right) the spell-check won't help. The spell-check can't tell if you meant *its* or *it's*; *their, they're,* or *there*; *affect* or *effect*; or *whether* or *weather*. Even the grammar check may not catch some problems. In addition, the grammar check may suggest you correct things that aren't wrong. Make use of these features, but again, don't rely on them entirely.

Be sure that your subjects and verbs agree. If one is plural, both must be. Ditto your nouns and pronouns. Don't use plural pronouns with singular nouns, or vice versa. If you are talking about one person, you must use *he* or *she*, not *they*. While we frequently use *they* to avoid sexist language, make sure the *they* refers to a plural noun.

Don't misspell the names of the authors or theories you refer to. The spell-check probably won't catch them, so double-check. From an instructor's point of view, it is a terrible sign of carelessness to have a student write about Locke or contractarianism, for example, and continually misspell the names. The first time you refer to an author, use his whole name. Yes, your instructor knows to whom you are referring, but do it anyway. Also, be sure when you say, "Locke said . . .," that it is really something Locke said and not something someone else claims Locke said.

Finally, choose a title that is descriptive of your essay. Your title should suggest the subject of your essay in a way that arouses the reader's interest. However, use common sense. If you title your essay about Mill's *Utilitarianism* "Pig Philosophy," it will catch your reader's interest, but it may not be the kind of interest you want. Titles should be relatively short, somewhat interesting, and indicative of what follows in the essay.

MECHANICS

After you have finished revising and editing your essay, you need to prepare it to be handed in. If your instructor has given you instructions, *follow them!* How you staple the pages or what kind of paper you use may seem like minor issues, but after all, the person who is grading your essay is the person who made those requests—so humor her!

If you don't own or have access to a computer, consider using the school's computer lab. Preparing a paper on a computer is much easier than typing it on a typewriter. If you use the computer lab, don't wait until the last minute to try to type your paper. Some computer labs require you to sign up in advance. Also, there are many times during the semester when the lab will be especially busy (midterms, finals, etc.). Be sure you sign up far enough in advance so that if there are scheduling problems, you can resolve them.

If your instructor has not given you specific instructions, follow these guidelines. Use 8½ X 11-inch white paper. Do not use erasable typewriter paper, other extremely thin paper, or paper in fancy colors or finishes. Make sure your typewriter or printer ribbon is printing clearly. Do not use colored ribbons. Double-space everything. Indent paragraphs five spaces.

Prepare a title page that includes your title, the course name, the instructor's name, the date, and your name. Most instructors have essays from several courses to grade. Having the course name on the title page simplifies matters for the instructor. If your instructor teaches more than one section of the same course, be sure to include the section number and the day and time your class meets, as well. Number all pages except the title page, including the bibliography, endnotes, and/or reference list, if any. It is also helpful to have your name on every page—in case one page becomes separated from the rest of the paper.

Use one-inch margins all around. Don't use huge margins in hopes that your instructor will be deceived into thinking your essay is longer than it is. Similarly, don't try to compress a long paper with small type and smaller line spacing. Don't use very large type or very small type—stick with 10- or 12-point type. Shoot for about 250–300 words per page.

Stay within the limits the instructor has set. If your essay is too short, go back and do some rewriting to bring it up to the length specified. If it is too long, cut out extraneous material. Your instructor has asked for a particular length essay because she thinks that this length is necessary to say all that needs to be said without rambling.

Unless the instructor specifies differently, staple the pages together in the upper left-hand corner. Don't use pins or paper clips or expect the instructor to supply you with staples. Use a plain, ordinary typeface. Script and other fancy typefaces can be very difficult to read. Don't use folders or fancy bindings unless the instructor specifically requests them. Your instructor will not confuse an attractive paper with a well-written one. At best, she will ignore the fancy binding or typeface—at worst, they will be a source of annoyance or distraction to her.

Proofread your essay one last time before you hand it in. Make sure the pages are in the right order and are numbered correctly. If you find errors, correct them carefully with a black pen. Be sure you keep a copy of your essay—not only on the computer, but on paper, too. If you've typed your essay, then photocopy it. Essays sometimes get lost, even by instructors.

Hand in your essay on time. If you know you will be late, speak to your instructor before the essay is due, if possible. Don't have your mother or your roommate call for you to make excuses. When your essay is returned—study it. Try to understand why you received the grade you did. Before you go to the instructor with complaints, however, wait at least 24 hours. Review what you wrote, the original work that you were writing about, and any comments or instructions from the instructor. Then, if you still have questions, make an appointment to meet with the instructor. Be sure to bring the essay with you—you can't expect her to remember all the details. Finally, good luck. If you have followed all (or most) of the advice in this and earlier chapters, then you will have made your own luck

Appendix A

HOW TO TAKE EXAMS

There are two very important things to remember when taking an exam. First and most important is this: **STUDY for the exam**. Second, **read through the entire exam before you try to answer any questions**. A student told me once about an exam she had recently taken. There were a number of extremely difficult essay questions, which she struggled to answer in the time allotted. When she got to the last page, however, the instructor had written, "Answer only one of the preceding questions." Oops! The few minutes you spend reading over the exam are well spent for that reason, as for several others.

Other suggestions to keep in mind at exam time follow.

Read the Instructions Very Carefully

Your instructor may ask you to answer five of eight short answer questions, or two of three essay questions. You will not get extra credit for answering more (unless the instructor explicitly says so), so don't waste your time. On the other hand, be sure you answer as many as required. If you don't attempt to answer at least five of the eight, then you may lose a significant number of points.

Budget Your Time

You need to know how many points each section or question of the exam is worth. If one question is worth 50 percent of the total number of points, plan to spend half your time answering that question. If another question is only worth 10 percent of the total, you would be foolish to waste too much time on it. Figure out how much time you have to spend on each section or question, and then budget your time. If you must, stop writing when you've used up the time for that question, and move on to the next one. In general, you will get a better score if you answer all the questions at least partially than if you answer only a few completely.

Briefly Outline What You Plan to Say

For example, here is a sample question:

> We talked about several possible exceptions to the principle of autonomy. What are they? For each exception, provide an explanation of what a person who held that principle would say about legalizing prostitution.

A scratch outline might look like this:

I. Define autonomy
II. Define exceptions:
    A. Paternalism
    B. Harm principle
    C. Welfare principle
    D. Legal moralism
III. Legalized prostitution
    A. Principle of paternalism—no
    B. Harm principle—yes
    C. Welfare principle—maybe yes or no
    D. Legal moralism principle—no

By making a quick outline, you insure not only that your essay is somewhat organized, but also that you answer everything asked. I have used this question on several exams, and almost inevitably, several people answer everything except the part about legalized prostitution. That is a big part of the answer I expect, because applying the principles to the issue of prostitution shows me how well the student actually understands those principles.

Think Before You Write

Read all the questions and answer the one you know most about first (but be sure to keep your eye on the clock, so you don't spend too much time on it). While you are answering the questions you are most sure of, your subconscious may be working on the others. Also, answering one question may spark something relevant about one of the others.

Answer the Question That Is Asked

If your instructor asks you to define a term, define that term. Don't define some other term or pad your answer with related but irrelevant information. Answer the question asked, and make sure you answer the entire question. Essay questions often have several parts, and if you answer only the first part, you will automatically lose points. So be sure you read the entire question carefully.

Use Your Outline to Write Your Answer

Because you are under a time constraint, you will not be able to write the kind of essay you could write out of class. Among other things, that means you should probably forget about any introduction or conclusion. Jump right in with the answer. For example, for the earlier question on exceptions to the principle of autonomy, your essay should probably begin something like this: "According to the principle of autonomy . . ." You can't write a perfect essay in 15 minutes or even in 50 minutes. Your instructor does not expect it. He does expect you to answer every required question, and every part of each question. He also expects that your exam will be readable—so don't write so carelessly that he can't decipher it. In addition, you need to pay attention to grammar, because although he will not expect it to be letter-perfect, he will expect it to be coherent.

Don't Worry About Revising or Editing

You may not have time to revise or edit. Try not to stop in mid-sentence, but do move on to the next question when the time you have allotted is up, so that each question is at least partially answered. Most instructors give partial credit on essay exams, so writing something is almost always better than writing nothing. If you really don't know the answer—guess. It is better to try rather than not. Go back and revise after you have answered all the questions, if you have time. It is a good idea, when you are deciding on how many minutes to devote to each question, to give yourself a little leeway of five minutes or more. Those few minutes should give you time to proofread your answers. When you are under time pressure, it is easy to leave out words, to write down one name when you mean another, and to misspell words and names. It is better to spend a little less time on each question, in order to use the time saved to proofread.

Don't Pad Your Answers, but Do Include Relevant Examples

Even if the instructor doesn't ask for an example, giving a brief one can help to show that you understand the concepts. Try not to use the same examples your book uses or that your instructor has used in class. Again, if the question on autonomy had not referred to legalized prostitution but had asked only for definitions, including a brief example when you define each principle could help show you know what you are talking about. Here is a relevant piece of the answer to that question:

The principle of paternalism says that we can violate a person's autonomy in order to prevent him from doing something that will harm himself. For example, a person who accepts paternalism would be in favor of preventing people from committing suicide. The harm principle says that we can stop people from doing things, if what they are doing is going to harm someone else. So a person in favor of the harm principle would be in favor of preventing rapes, murders, and assaults.

Notice that the examples are very short, but long enough to demonstrate that you know how to apply the principle.

Use Your Own Words to Express the Ideas

Sometimes, you have heard a particular principle so many times that you can quote it verbatim. For example, once learned, most students can quote the principle of utility: "An action is right in proportion as it tends to promote happiness and wrong as it tends to produce unhappiness." That isn't a direct quote (quite), but it is very, very close to the original. If you are asked what the principle of utility is, and that is all you say, your instructor has no way of knowing if you understand what it means. Put it into your own words, and provide examples. You may have to use more words than the original principle and it may not sound as elegant, but it will provide your instructor with a much better idea of whether you understand what you are writing.

Bring and Use the Kind of Pencil or Pen Your Instructor Requests

If he does not tell you beforehand, bring both pencil and pen. Use only blue or black ink—fancy colors are distracting and can be hard to read. Plus, if you write in pink or red, then the instructor's notes and corrections may not show up very well. Plan to bring paper to the exam, even if the instructor doesn't tell you that you will need it. If the instructor requires that you use a blue book, bring at least one and preferably two or three, in case you need more space or some other problem develops.

Be as Neat as You Can Be

Since you are writing under a time constraint, your instructor won't expect perfection. However, she will expect that your exam will be easily readable. If you use paper to write your essay questions, instead of a blue book, make sure you staple the pages together in the right order. After answering a question, leave the rest of the page blank so that if you need to add something to it later, you'll have room. If you must mark out a sentence or paragraph that you don't want in your answer, mark it clearly and completely by drawing a single line through it; don't scribble all over it and make a mess trying to hide what it says. If you are allowed to use pencil, do! That way you can erase mistakes instead of marking them out.

Show Up for Class on the Day Your Instructor
Returns and Discusses the Exam

Look over the exam carefully to discover what you did right and what you did wrong. Don't simply look at the grade and then throw it away. Keep the exam at least until you get your final grade for the class. If you have any questions about your exam or about any comments the instructor made on it, make an appointment to see him to go over it. But before you do that, go back and compare your exam to the text to see if you can figure out for yourself what you did wrong and why.

Finally, Don't Panic

An exam is simply an exam, and in most classes a bad grade on one exam will not cause you to flunk the class. A poor performance on an exam does not mean you are a terrible person, that you are going to fail the course, or that you will never achieve true happiness. Keep it in perspective. It is just an exam.

Appendix B

USEFUL POLITICAL SCIENCE SOURCES

Specialized Dictionaries

This should be the first resource you consult when you begin to look for references. There are many dictionaries of political science available. Which ones your library has is anyone's guess. Available dictionaries include dictionaries of international biography, history of ideas, political philosophy, American government, political science, etc.

Encyclopedias

There are a number of encyclopedias available that cover political science, government, foreign affairs, political thought and many other areas that might be useful to the political science student. Again, go to the library and look. Check the card catalog under Political Science—Encyclopedias and Dictionaries. Be aware that some of these encyclopedias will be too difficult for introductory students. If you don't understand what you are reading, try another encyclopedia. Or go to a good specialized dictionary and read the reference in it, to see if it helps you understand the encyclopedia reference better. Browse the reference section to see what else is available.

Internet Resources

Most government agencies have web sites, as do the White House, the Senate, and Congress. Many universities have excellent information available, especially the law schools. Also, there are a number of private organizations and news agencies that make a great deal of information available. Your best bet is to go hunting using a good search engine. Keep in mind when you use Internet resources both timeliness and the discussion in Chapter 8 about evaluating resources. Especially if you are writing about a current policy or situation, you need to check to see how recently the web site was updated.

Journals of Political Science

Journals are published regarding practically every topic or subfield in political science. Again, what is available to you in your college library will vary. Most of these journals are indexed in *The Social Sciences Index*, which is available in quarterly volumes or on CD-ROM. In addition, the Index catalogs books, book reviews, anthologies, and individual articles from anthologies. Each book or article is indexed by both subject and author. Before you go to the Index, however, check to see what journals your library carries. Many libraries carry only a limited selection of journals, so don't waste your time discovering great references in the Index, only to find that you don't have access to the right journals.

Journals are filled with articles written by professional scholars for other professional scholars. That is, very few of them are geared toward undergraduate students, and many of the articles may be too difficult to understand. Find which journals your library carries and go check out a couple of issues. If they are too difficult, ignore them. Some articles in some journals may not be too difficult, so you might want to at least try. Don't give up without at least checking.

Introductory Texts

One good source to start with may be an introductory text. In fact, if your library resources are limited in the way of dictionaries, encyclopedias, or historical texts, you may have to rely on introductory texts. Many of them are anthologies of primary sources, which often have explanatory introductions to the readings. An even greater number of introductory texts are secondary sources that explain to you what the arguments, policies, and theories are, and what different people have said about them. However, see Chapter 8 on the subject of evaluating sources. All introductory texts are not created equal, so don't accept that any one particular text is correct. If you find the same material in several places, then you can be more confident that the source is accurate.

Logic Texts

If you need more help on deductive and inductive arguments, informal and formal fallacies, emotive language, and the like, try one of these books:

Patrick J. Hurley, A Concise Introduction to Logic, 6th ed. (Belmont, CA: Wadsworth Publishing Company, 1997).

S. Morris Engel, With Good Reason: An Introduction to Informal Fallacies, 4th ed. (New York: St. Martin's Press, 1990).

Howard Kahane, Logic and Contemporary Rhetoric: The Use of Reason in Everyday Life, 6th ed. (Belmont, CA: Wadsworth Publishing Company, 1992).

Appendix C

GLOSSARY

analogy An "argument by analogy" claims that since two things are similar in some ways, they are similar in some other important, significant way.

analysis Reducing a complex whole (like an argument) into its simpler, component parts.

appeal to authority Claiming that a statement is true on the basis of what some authority says.

appeal to unqualified authority A fallacy that occurs when the "authority" cited is not an authority on that subject.

application To apply a theory, argument, or principle to a new situation or scenario.

argument A group of statements (called premises), one or more of which claim to provide proof, support, and/or reasons to believe another statement (called the conclusion).

argumentative essay One in which some argument is presented—either an original argument in favor of some conclusion, or an argument explaining why some argument is wrong (see Chapters 6 and 7).

Aristotle (384–322 B.C.) Greek philosopher, student of Plato.

assumption Something we take to be true, without any argument or justification.

autonomy The idea that people should be allowed to make their own choices, to choose the kind of person they want to be and the kind of life they want to lead, to be self-determining, without interference from others. We violate a person's autonomy when we prevent him

94

from doing what he wants to do and/or force him to do something that he does not want to do.

bibliography A list of all the books or articles consulted or referred to in an essay or article.

capital punishment The practice of executing prisoners who have committed crimes that are considered to be appropriately punishable by death.

capitalism An economic system in which the means of production and distribution are privately owned and operated for profit.

citation A footnote, endnote, or parenthetical reference giving credit to the person whose words or ideas are used.

cogent A cogent inductive argument is one that is strong and has true premises.

communism The theory that advocates a classless society, where each person works according to his abilities and receives goods and services according to his needs. Also opposes ownership of private property.

conclusion What the premises in an argument are supposed to be providing proof or support for.

counter-argument An opposing argument to show why some other argument is wrong.

counter-example An example used to show that some argument, principle, or theory is wrong by substituting terms that make the premises true and the conclusion false.

deductive argument An argument in which the premises are claimed to support the conclusion in such a way that if all the premises are true, then the conclusion must also be true.

democracy The form of government in which the people themselves, or their elected representatives, hold the political power to create laws, run the government, etc.

dilemma Strictly speaking, a dilemma involves a situation where you have only two incompatible choices, and both seem to be obligatory. In addition, both may be equally unattractive for some reason. For example, when telling the truth would cause harm to someone but telling a lie also seems to be wrong, you are caught "between the horns" of the dilemma. For example, see the homicidal maniac case.

distributive justice Theory for determining the appropriate distribution of the benefits and burdens of society.

Electoral College Electors who meet to determine the presidential and vice-presidential election.

emotional language Language that expresses feelings or emotions and intends to induce those feelings in the reader or listener.

endnote A citation found at the end of a chapter or book.

equivocate Using a word or phrase to mean two different things.

ethics One of the main branches of philosophy which studies right and wrong, good and bad.

evaluation Providing your opinion of how good or bad an argument is, along with reasons for why you think so.

example An instance that illustrates a principle, argument, or theory. In the previous definition (of the evil genius), "1 + 1 = 2" was an example of the kinds of things Descartes thought the evil genius might be deceiving him about.

existentialism School of philosophy that emphasizes both freedom and responsibility. Existentialists claim that we are totally free (as in never being caused to act by heredity, environment, or personality) and thus we alone are responsible for our actions.

expediency Suitable for achieving a particular desired result. When John Stuart Mill talks about actions being "expedient," he means that they will result in happiness.

fact A fact is usually seen in opposition to a belief or an opinion. A fact is something that can be proved, for which supporting documentation can be produced. A belief or opinion cannot be proved in the same way. When a fetus's brain begins to develop is a fact; whether or not it is right to abort a fetus is an opinion.

fallacy A fallacy is a mistake made in an argument. Usually it is one that seems correct but isn't, often because of ambiguities in grammar, the meanings of words, or the inclination to be convinced by reasons that are not good ones.

false cause fallacy A fallacy that occurs when the conclusion of an argument depends on a causal connection that probably doesn't exist.

false dichotomy or false dilemma fallacy A fallacy that occurs when only two alternatives are presented, but in fact some third alternative is possible.

feminism, feminist A group of philosophical theories (usually political and/or ethical) that (1) are largely based on the premise that at least some parts of our society are exploitive of and unjust to women and (2) advocate change.

footnote A citation found at the bottom of the page on which the words or ideas are cited.

formal fallacy A mistake in reasoning that occurs because there is something wrong with the form or structure of the argument.

gender-specific Usually, the use of masculine pronouns when talking about groups of people that include both men and women.

greatest happiness principle John Stuart Mill's ethical theory (utilitarianism) which states that the right action is the one that leads to the greatest amount of happiness for the greatest number of people.

harm principle The principle that we may violate a person's autonomy in order to prevent him from harming other people.

inductive argument An argument in which the premises are claimed to support the conclusion in such a way that if the premises are true, the conclusion is probably true as well.

informal fallacy A mistake in reasoning that is not a matter of the form or structure of the argument, but can only be identified by examining the content of the argument.

interest group Group of individuals who form an alliance to influence policy.

invalid deductive argument A deductive argument in which it is possible for all the premises to be true and the conclusion to be false (having to do with the form of the argument).

is/ought fallacy A mistake in reasoning that occurs when the arguer moves from saying that something is the case to saying that it ought to be the case.

justice Fairness and impartiality of treatment; also, the idea that people should get what they deserve.

justify, justification To justify a statement means to provide reasons and arguments to show that it is true.

legal moralism The idea that the purpose of the law is to enforce morality. Thus we can violate a person's autonomy any time we think that what they are about to do is immoral.

Locke, John (1632–1704) English empiricist and political philosopher.

logic A branch of philosophy that is concerned with correct reasoning and the evaluation of arguments.

Marcuse, Herbert (1898-1979) American Marxist Political Philosopher.

Marx, Karl (1818–1883) German philosopher and social theorist. Known for his theory of communism.

Milgram's experiment Stanley Milgram's experiment on reliance on authority, testing subjects willingness to follow orders even to the point of causing great harm to others..

Mill, John Stuart (1806–1873) English philosopher. Known primarily for his doctrine of utilitarianism.

moral theory See ethics.

Mussolini, Benito (1883–1945) Italian fascist premier.

necessary A "necessary truth" is a statement that must be true—that cannot be false. A "necessary condition" is one that has to be true in order for something else to be true. For example, being an animal is a necessary condition for being a dog, because nothing is a dog, unless it is also an animal.

necessary conclusion In a deductive argument, a conclusion is necessary when the argument is valid and all the premises are true.

night-watchman state Robert Nozick's theory of the minimal kind of government which only protects individuals from interference with rights to property.

Nozick, Robert (1938-) American Political Philosopher..

opinion A belief that is not supported by evidence. Contrast with fact.

parenthetical reference Used instead of footnotes or endnotes to cite a source. For example: (Descartes 13). Used after the quotation marks but before the period.

paraphrase To put the ideas from a sentence or passage into your own words.

parliamentary government A democracy in which the executive and legislative functions reside in one body—the parliament.

paternalism The principle that we may violate a person's autonomy in order to prevent him from harming himself.

philosophy Comes from Greek words meaning "love of wisdom." In general, it is a field of study (like biology or mathematics) in which what is studied are the most basic principles—Does God exist? What is time? Who am I? What is good? Includes such subfields as ethics, epistemology, metaphysics, etc.

plagiarism Using someone else's words or ideas in such a way as to imply that they are your own.

Plato (428?–?348 B.C.) Ancient Greek philosopher, student of Socrates. His writings are some of the first attempts to answer the questions of philosophy.

political philosophy The branch of philosophy that is concerned with what the right kind of government is and various other political issues.

premise The reasons, evidence, and/or justifications given to show that a conclusion is true.

primary sources A primary source is an author's own writing about a topic. A secondary source is one that explains what an author said about the topic. So a primary source is by the author, and the secondary source is about the author and/or his arguments.

principle of charity When we read an author's words, we should interpret them in such a way that makes them most likely to be true and plausible.

principle of utility See utilitarianism.

probable conclusion When a conclusion is probable, it means that you can't be absolutely certain that it is true—it is only probably true. See inductive argument.

proof A proof or demonstration of a statement is a sound/cogent argument with that statement as the conclusion. See also argument.

quotation When you use an author's exact words. Note that they should be surrounded by quotation marks (" ").

reference list A list of all the books, articles, essays, etc. that have been cited in parenthetical references in the body of an essay.

research paper Any paper for which you are expected to find and read material from sources other than your textbook.

rhetoric Persuasive, flamboyant, or elaborate language. Usually used in contrast to genuine argument, implying that it is mere persuasion, without reasons and evidence to back it up.

Sartre, Jean-Paul (1905–1980) French philosopher. Known primarily for his theory of existentialism.

secondary sources See primary sources.

sexist To show attitudes involving discrimination and oppression on the basis of sex.

socialism A theory that advocates a classless society and public ownership of the means of production, but which is distinguished from communism by the fact that benefits and burdens of society are unequally distributed according to the individual's contribution to society.

Socrates (470?–399 B.C.) Greek philosopher whose ideas were recorded by Plato. Extremely influential because of his "Socratic dialogue"—a method of discovering the truth by a series of questions and answers.

sound A sound deductive argument is one in which the argument form is valid and all the premises are true.

straw man fallacy A fallacy in which an argument is caricatured or misrepresented in order to make it easy to refute.

strong inductive argument An argument in which the premises provide only probable support for the conclusion. Thus the conclusion is not guaranteed to be true; it is only more likely to be true than it is to be false.

summary An attempt to put the main ideas and arguments of an essay or passage into one's own words. Distinguished from paraphrase by the fact that a summary is usually considerably shorter than the original and is concerned with only the most important points of the essay.

superscript A small letter or number that is placed above the level of the other words. For example:^{3}.

syntax The way words are put together to form phrases and sentences; having to do with the grammar or form of a sentence.

synthesis A synthesis essay brings together parts and elements of several theories to create a new whole that requires original thinking.

term Usually a noun or a noun phrase, which can be used as the subject of a sentence.

thesis A thesis statement is usually the conclusion of an argument—that is, it is the idea that an essay argues for or tries to establish.

thesis defense essay An essay in which the writer takes a position and defends it.

uncogent inductive argument An inductive argument in which either one or more of the premises are false or the argument form is weak, or both.

understanding essay An essay meant to show not only that you know a particular concept or theory, but also that you understand what it means.

Unger, Roberto (1947 -) Brazilian law professor and political theorist.

unsound deductive argument A deductive argument in which either one or more of the premises are false or the argument form is invalid, or both.

utilitarianism The ethical theory that states that an action's rightness or wrongness depends upon whether the consequences of the action lead to happiness or unhappiness. A morally right action is one that produces happiness, and a morally wrong action is one that produces unhappiness.

utility For a philosopher, it means more than just usefulness; it means the amount of happiness something produces. See utilitarianism.

valid deductive argument An argument that has a structure or form such that whenever the premises are true, the conclusion must also be true.

weak inductive argument An inductive argument whose premises do not provide good reasons for thinking the conclusion is even probably true.

welfare principle The principle that we may violate a person's autonomy in order to force him to help other people